What Wendell Wants

Also by Jenny Lee

I DO. I DID. NOW WHAT?!:
Life After the Wedding Dress

Jenny Lee

DELACORTE PRESS

What Wendell Wants

or, How to Tell If You're Obsessed with Your Dog

WHAT WENDELL WANTS
or, How to Tell If You're Obsessed with Your Dog
A Delacorte Book / September 2004

Published by Bantam Dell
A division of Random House, Inc.
New York, New York

Book design by Lynn Newmark
Illustration of Wendell on title page by Laura Hartman Maestro

Library of Congress Cataloging in Publication Data is on file with the publisher.

ISBN: 0-385-33785-X

Manufactured in the United States of America
Published simultaneously in Canada

10   9   8   7   6   5   4   3   2   1
BVG

In loving memory of my father, Seung H. Lee,
who gave me my first puppy

CONTENTS

(Please Answer Questions Below with Yes or No)

ANSWER KEY
(Score based on number of "yes" answers)

1-2 Your dog may not be getting enough attention
3-4 You seem to have a healthy appreciation for your dog
5-7 Yes, others might call you obsessed
8-9 You've really crossed the line
10 True love (dysfunctional, of course, but more power to you both!)

What Wendell Wants

INTRODUCTION

Obsessed? Who, Me?...

You know, dog obsession is a funny thing. First off, most people who are obsessed probably don't even know it. Sure, their friends have been quietly suggesting for months (or perhaps years) that "you might be getting a little *too* attached to that dog," but what could they possibly know?

Then there are the dog owners who might have an inkling of their tendencies, but feel slightly defensive about it ("Well, yes, as a matter of fact I *do* read *Where the Red Fern Grows* out loud to my puppy, but how is that anyone's business but mine?").

And *then*, there are the people who not only fully realize that they're obsessed with their dog, but also simply accept it (I call this Stage 3)—and in fact take a certain amount of pride in their affliction.

Back in the dark ages before I was obsessed with my own

dog (B.W., or Before Wendell), I, too, made fun of my friends and the crazy things they'd do in the name of their dogs. Take my friends John and Stephanie: They spent six nights camping out on their floor in sleeping bags after their beagle, Emma, got spayed and was temporarily unable to jump on and off their bed due to stitches. I mean, *hardwood* floors! "But after all," they explained, "Emma was used to sleeping with us, so what else could we do?" I remember laughing to myself, thinking, *Why not just rig up some sort of hydraulic platform lift?* Which I hesitated to say, since there was a very good chance John might actually pursue it—I mean, he did go to MIT. . . .

And what about the guy who had his apartment custom-designed and furnished to cater to his two miniature dachshunds—making sure that the steps from the living room were half the normal size to accommodate his dogs' stubby little legs. Or the standard, dime-a-dozen stories: people taking their dogs out for completely gratuitous car rides each day, just so they have a chance to take in the scenery; cooking Cordon Bleu meals for their dogs nightly, and baking cakes for them on special occasions; waiting in line at Petco for hours each Christmas just so they can get a picture of their little one sitting on Santa's lap (next year's card, of course) . . .

But now, in the new millennium (A.W., or After Wendell), I no longer laugh. Because I know this obsession from the inside out. Trust me. When Wendell was neutered last year on Valentine's Day (a slight scheduling gaffe, obviously) and I just couldn't bear to leave him home alone in pain, I actually canceled our insanely hard-to-get reservations at Lumiere.

(Having spent hours on the phone trying to get us in, my husband, Cosmas, was none too pleased, but I assured him that he'd get to keep all the points he won for "planning ahead," plus a few bonus points for being such a good sport about canceling our plans—not to mention the fact that he was now saving himself about two hundred bucks in the bargain. . . . In fact, now that I think of it, maybe *I* should have been getting a few points. But I digress. . . .)

These days I feel I can even understand all those people who have been Stage 3 types for so long, they've entered into a classification all their own—which I'll refer to as TOWD (or, Totally Obsessed With Dog). You see, for TOWDs, obsession is no longer just a state of mind, but an actual lifestyle. You know, head-to-toe dog stuff, 24/7—the doggie sweatshirt . . . the schnauzer socks . . . the lapel pins shaped like one's breed of choice, with those little jeweled eyes . . . This is not one cute doggie mug, or the occasional puppy calendar. No, TOWDs have full *services* of doggie china . . . kitchen clocks with little toy poodles and miniature pinschers instead of numbers . . . doggie wallpaper in the foyer bathroom, doggie cross-stitch patterns framed and hanging in their living room, and maybe some of those dog bookends with the smoking-jacketed hound sitting in a wing chair, reading a book. . . .

Now, I'm hardly a card-carrying TOWD yet, but I *have* been secretly eyeing this adorable dog-head napkin dispenser (it'd be a done deal if they had a wheaten terrier one). And I have to recognize the fact that coveting this napkin dispenser suggests that my dog mania may still be evolving. Perhaps someday in the not-so-distant future, Cosmas, Wendell, and I will find ourselves walking down our street (we live on Wendell Street, which we now tell people was named for our dog, as opposed to the other way around) decked out in matching "canine chic" sweat suits, oblivious to all the stares and the whispers. . . . It is, after all, a slippery slope.

So, what do people do if they think they might know someone (a friend of a friend—not themselves, of course) who might be dog obsessed? Is there some preventive measure people can take? *Is* there a cure for dog obsession?

The simple answer is no.

Your best bet is simply not to try and fight it. But perhaps it will be some consolation to know you're not alone.

And, with that in mind . . .

Do You Talk About Your Dog Nonstop?

THIRTY-ONE WAYS TO GET A DOG

It all started one evening with one of my melodramatic pronouncements: "Something's missing from our lives," I said. My husband, Cosmas, reading a science journal appropriately enough named *Science,* was sitting on the couch just across the room, but did nothing to indicate he'd heard my pronouncement. Of course, Cosmas knows me almost too well by now, and has come to expect melodrama and has been trying out ways to avoid it. A few seconds later, just as I was about to repeat myself in a louder voice, perhaps to be followed by a pillow chaser adroitly aimed for the magazine in his hands, he let out a quiet "Mmmmmm?" which meant he was now at least pretending to listen, so there would be no need for pillow violence.

I released the pillow I was clutching, gave a deep sigh, and continued: "It's just that I feel there is a void in our life." I paused for effect here. "A chasm really." Cosmas's eyes began scanning the page faster, desperately trying to get to the end of the paragraph about nucleotides he'd been immersed in. Because everyone knows—well, at least *he* did, after a healthy dose of trial and error—that one pronouncement followed by another increasingly serious pronouncement requires immediate attention. (It's like one of those SAT verbal questions—*MISSING* is to *VOID* as *CHASM* is to *PAY ATTENTION OR RISK UNTIMELY DEATH BY SOFA PILLOW!*) Of course, the tricky thing for Cosmas to figure out has always been when I'm just a little bored at the moment, and simply "sharing" my thoughts with him, versus those times when he actually needs to take me seriously (for instance, when I'm talking about gaping black holes in our so-called life).

When I had finally won his undivided attention (by walking over to him and snatching away his magazine), I looked him straight in the eye and asked, "Do *you* feel that there is something missing in our lives?" This is where, had he been wearing a collared shirt, he would have unbuttoned the top button to make room for the slam dunk of his Adam's apple as he gulped it down to the back of his throat. Instead he did a quick preemptive rub of his temples, trying to ward away the nervous sweat beads just breaking through his skin (actually this was a rather nice combination move, in which the whole gesture moved smoothly into the ol' playin'-it-casual, runnin'-my-fingers-through-my-hair thing).

Of course, he assumed I was thinking B-A-B-Y (I assume

he would have tried to spell the word out in his head, sort of the way he'd previously spelled out M-A-R-R-I-A-G-E, in that typically guy leap of logic that saying a word out loud will somehow make it more of a reality). After all, we'd been married for over two years now. He probably also realized it was the third week of the month, signifying two important things that never seemed to work in his favor:

First, my emotions were running high due to PMS. And second, this "delicate emotional state" (which was how Cosmas referred to a woman's sudden ability to slam a pint of ice cream in five minutes) happened to coincide with what I referred to as "the Dead Zone." I'm a certifiable magazine junkie, and the Dead Zone is that time of the month (usually the third week) when I've already read all the current month's fashion mags and am waiting for the new ones to hit the stands. This can last anywhere between two and five days, and it generally isn't pretty (Cosmas and I have discussed the merits of reworking my Pill cycle to separate these two events for the sake of my own sanity and the well-being of those around me [i.e., Cosmas], but as it was decided that the risk of fooling around with the Pill [i.e., risk of B-A-B-Y] was the greater of two evils, we've left things as they are).

Another reason he would have thought I was thinking B-A-B-Y was because I had been (purposely) chattering nonstop about how much fun it was to shop for baby stuff, as one of my closest friends just had her first baby. Every night for the previous week during dinner, I'd managed to find an opening to talk about baby stuff. Cosmas would finish telling me about some protein that he thought might be part of the equation when it comes to eye formation, and I'd say something like, "You know, speaking of eyes, did you know that all babies' eyes start out blue, and only later change to their final color after a few weeks?" He'd sort of freeze for a moment, and then I'd laugh a bit too loudly and say, "DUH, of course you know that—you're a doctor. You know all about babies, right?" Then, much to his relief, I'd drop the subject completely.

This was merely the groundwork for my master plan, and, of course, the damage would already have been done. Cosmas would push his plate aside and claim that he was suddenly full.

Of course, I wasn't thinking about a B-A-B-Y at all—oh, no, we were far from ready to cross that particular bridge. Human babies wouldn't even be on the radar for at least another two years, and by then I was pretty sure that both of our mothers would be willing to throw out large cash incentives (I was hoping for a new car, personally). No, the whole B-A-B-Y thing was a means to a totally different end.

"It's just that I think it's the right time in our lives," I announced. "And we're ready, well, at least *I'm* ready. You're ready, too, right?!" Cosmas's eyes widened in terror at the thought that having a B-A-B-Y in the house would give him even less quiet time to read his science journals, and for a split second I thought the whole thing was about to backfire, as he appeared to be on the verge of blacking out.

So I blurted it out in hopes that his head would nod forward in a way that could later be interpreted as a yes just before he slumped to the floor.

"I think we should get a puppy!"

Cosmas let out a noisy sigh of relief, so happy to be wrong about the B-A-B-Y that he almost said, "Sure, whatever you want, dear." Then he stopped himself short and made a face that said, "Not so fast, woman—I've fallen for your bait-and-switch routines one too many times" (like the time I pretended to be really interested in a three-thousand-dollar Cartier watch when all I was really after was a grossly overpriced special-edition plastic Hello Kitty watch that was over a hundred bucks).

Hmmmm . . . Who knew that husbands actually *do* get smarter with time? Drats.

I moved swiftly to ensure that I'd stay on the offensive, speaking fast and furious:

"You *promised* that I could get a puppy. *Remember* how I said that a *dog* was a marriage *deal breaker?* You *swore* that after we got married we could get one. *Two years* we've been married, and I've waited long enough. I want one. I want one. I want one." I stamped my foot for emphasis in case he couldn't already tell that I was taking the defiant-five-year-old approach.

He scratched his head thoughtfully and opened his mouth to speak, but then closed it again without saying anything.

Clearly he had forfeited his turn to speak, so I continued on course: "Please can we get a puppy? Please. Pleeeaaaase!

Pretty please? Pretty please with thirty-one flavors of ice cream and a cherry on top? I'll *name* them. Chocolate; strawberry; rocky road; mint chip; Heath bar crunch; strawberry shortcake; peanut-butter praline swirl; coffee mocha chip; that one with the dark chocolate fishies and marshmallow stuff . . . how many is that? One, two, three . . ." I looked over at Cosmas, who was just sitting there, torturing me with his silence. Surely he wasn't really going to be such a baby and make me name all thirty-one flavors. I mean, it's really just a figure of speech. Oh, well, fine—two could play at this game. . . . "Chocolate chip; cookie dough; green tea; lime sherbet; rainbow sherbet . . ."

"Is sherbet the same thing as ice cream?" he asked in all seriousness.

I ignored him and continued, "Lemon chiffon; bovinity divinity; fudge royale . . . You *do* know that if I name all these flavors, we *will* be getting a puppy . . . rum raisin . . ."

He sighed and finally said that I could stop now, and that perhaps that weekend . . . maaayybe he'd be willing to discuss the possibility of getting a puppy . . . one day . . . When in doubt, stall and throw in a lot of clauses in fine-point future conditional. I narrowed my eyes, annoyed at his stall tactics and continued, "Pistachio; butterscotch praline powwow; lady gives the finger, ahem . . . I mean, ladyfinger vanilla fandango; pecan peanut-brittle bonanza; Chunky Monkey . . ." Obviously I was now reaching, but I just *dared* him to challenge me.

He interrupted to ask why it was again that I wanted a puppy so badly. I said because I just wanted one, but if he needed specifics, then the main reason, in a nutshell, was that puppies were soft, furry, and always happy to see you whenever you come home. Cosmas cocked his head for a moment (sort of the way dogs do), and I knew that he must have been thinking that, based on that description alone, a puppy might very well put him out of a job, since that was pretty much the role he had been filling in our relationship. Then, as if reading cue cards, he coyly asked why I wanted a puppy when I already had all those things in a husband?

I told him it was different. Dogs were loyal. He countered that *he* was loyal. Dogs were sincere. He said he was nothing if not sincere. But best of all, I said with a certain satisfaction, dogs didn't work all the time. Cosmas said nothing. Next, I informed him that I thought it was really good practice for a baby (saying the word out loud just to watch him flinch). Dogs were a great stepping-stone on the path of responsibility and selflessness. Now he had to be wondering whether saying no to a puppy right now might just push me up the evolutionary ladder to request a B-A-B-Y.

I eyed his *Science* magazine longingly, probably wondering whether there was any chance at all he'd get to finish the article he was reading.

"Maple melon swirl; banana cream pie; periwinkle . . . okay, scratch that one as I think that's a Crayola Crayon color. . . ." I wondered whether it would be cheating if I actually called up Baskin-Robbins for a little help, sorta like my one Lifeline call. "Mango pineapple jubilee; cherry berry surprise; rigatoni ripple royale . . ."

Somewhere between flavors number twenty-eight and twenty-nine (veiled-threat-of-divorce vanilla and sleep-on-the-couch-forever fudge), he said "Okay," but I didn't hear him, as it was taking all my concentration to come up with a flavor that worked around the theme of changing the locks. . . .

So he decided to help me out with flavor thirty-one: "Okey-dokey Double-Dutch doggie delight," he suggested with a little smile.

Was this for real? Was Cosmas really finally truly ab-sosmurfly agreeing to getting a puppy? "You promise?" I screeched rather unbecomingly.

"I promise," he said, nodding. "Thirty-one flavors and a Milk-Bone on top."

Hooray—we were getting a dog! I was now doing my own version of an end-zone victory dance, and Cosmas got back to his magazine.

Good Manners Show Good Breeding: Ten Tips for Obsessed Dog Owners

1. Do not compare your dog's training, needs, and feelings to those of your friends' *human* children. Many seem to find this offensive. Better to make any such comparisons in your head and wait until later to tell your spouse or other close (nonparent) friend how much more advanced your Bitsy is than so-and-so's five-year-old.

2. When hosting people at your home, try not to mention that you let your dog eat off your plates, or that your husband finds it funny to let Skipper drink right out of the Brita water pitcher (like father, like dog), particularly if you go on to explain that you are trying to break Skipper from drinking out of the toilet.

3. Do not pick out your dog's eye crud and then flick it on the floor in front of other people (especially if you're in their house).

4. Make a point of indicating to people which chair or part of the couch is your dog's special place as soon as they enter,

so you won't have to ask anyone to get up later, in midconversation.

5. Keep in mind that other dog owners probably feel similarly to you; in other words, they, too, most likely see their dogs as special and smart in some singular way. Thus, it's probably best to tone down any boasting about your own dog, regardless of how justified.

6. Do not assume that if you've been invited to a dinner, barbecue, or an outdoor wedding that your dog has as well. The rule of thumb is that unless the dog's name is written on the envelope, he or she is probably *not* invited. The fact that you allowed people to bring their screaming children and/or weird boyfriends to your wedding must be accepted as irrelevant.

7. Subjects not appropriate for polite conversation in the human realm (e.g., bowel movements, flatulence, corpses) generally apply to dogs as well. So pointing out that your dog just farted and is now sniffing it should not be assumed as riotously funny to others as it may, in fact, be to you.

8. Though it may seem effective, make an effort not to discipline others in the same tone of voice you might use to discipline your dog.

9. Obviously, it is more than normal to talk to your dog when in the privacy of your own home, but when in the company of others (e.g., non–dog owners, disapproving relatives, cranky acquaintances), it is best to keep such intimate conversations to a minimum. The reason for this is that such people are likely to make fun of you to your face, saying things like "I can't believe you talk to your dog." Or "So does he talk back?" all the while laughing in a most unattractive way, which will of course not only offend you, but also, more importantly, may hurt the feelings of your dog.

10. When having tea with your dog, instruct him that it is impolite to eat the scones or tea sandwiches off the plate of the person next to him (or off the tea tray itself). Ha-ha, just joking! Everyone knows dogs don't like tea.

LOVE AT FIRST DOG

The first week with our new puppy was a total blur, but all in all it wasn't that bad. Sure, neither of us was getting much sleep—me, because little puppies come with little bladders (and ours also came with stomach problems), so I was up every three hours tromping down the stairs in my pajamas and a sweatshirt to stand around with a flashlight looking for yellow snow, and Cosmas, because he liked to sleep all wrapped around me and apparently standing outside in freezing weather had a tendency to make my skin cold. And once the sleep started to go then everything else soon followed suit, as I couldn't figure out how to keep an eagle eye on our new addition and do household chores at the same time, which meant that the apartment slowly went to hell. But I figured that eventually we'd all get on a schedule and things would soon normalize. I figured wrong.

It was the second week when the reality of how much our lives had changed finally sank in, when all the little practical details built up into the iceberg we would crash into. . . . I remember that I was sitting on the floor in front of our still-nameless puppy (a name, after all, is not something that should be taken lightly), placing two different types of kibble on the floor and trying to figure out which one he liked better (but what he ultimately preferred, it seemed, was pouncing on the kibble and then chasing after it as it skidded across the floor, issues of taste being less than relevant), when Cosmas walked into the kitchen and sat down at the kitchen table, holding a legal pad and a pen.

I looked over at him and just assumed his weird smile had something to do with some work computation he just figured out, as he had been huddled over my computer for the last hour or so, and so I said, "What's up?"

His small smile suddenly broke out into a full-gallop grin, and he said, "I've done some research this morning and I've drawn out three viable plans for LOTR and I wanted your feedback." He then held up his legal pad, which had the heading LOTR in caps across the top, and underneath it said Plan A, Plan B, and Plan C.

Having given up the kibble taste challenge—I was now just flicking kibble bits across the floor and watching the puppy chase them—I was only half listening and gave Cosmas the typically male response of "Uh-huh, whatever you say, honey."

"Jenny," Cosmas snapped, "this is important."

Obviously men can dish out flippant half answers, but they just can't take them. Something in the way he said my name, however (or maybe it was the fact that he used it at all, since I normally go by honey, sweetheart, or Bubba [don't ask]), made me stop midflick and look over at him.

"I'm sorry, what were you saying? You have my undivided attention now." This proved short-lived, however, as the puppy had begun to take on an expression suggesting that he was about to either pee or fall asleep in a way that might indicate a mild case of narcolepsy. . . . At this Cosmas stood up abruptly, knocking back the kitchen chair, grabbed his paper and pen, and proceeded to stomp off toward the bedroom, where he then heaved himself onto the bed with an exaggerated sigh.

I was more than a bit startled by this diva move, so reminiscent of my own, and it must have scared the puppy, too, as he came scrambling toward me, a clatter of puppy claws over slick hardwood. Elated that he clearly saw me as his protector, I scooped him into my arms and ran into the bedroom to share the news with Cosmas.

"Hey, guess what little pup just did?"

I got no response. "Cosmas?"

"I don't really give a crap what he did, but thanks for asking." Snarkiness, following a tantrum, is never a good sign, so I decided that telling him about the puppy's latest and greatest was not my wisest move.

I of course wanted to bring the puppy to the bed to help me solve the mystery of the cranky husband, but I figured that since the puppy wasn't even allowed on the bed to begin with (rule number one of Cosmas's DogLaws, as he calls them [which so doesn't work as a play on bylaws, but whatever]), I walked over to the blue crate sitting on the floor and tucked the pup into his little bed. Luckily he promptly curled up and went to sleep, and I proceeded to wish him a happy nappy and shut the door but didn't lock it.

I then attended to my wifely duty, which was to take a running start and make a flying leap onto the bed, landing right next to the grumpy lump with an enthusiastically whispered "Cowabunga!" (Didn't want to wake up you know who. . . .)

Cosmas rolled to his left, giving me the cold shoulder, and spoke into the pillow, which did serve to muffle some of the sarcasm: "Are you sure you have time to talk to me? Maybe you should go sing him a lullaby or something."

Suddenly all became clear, and it took everything I had to resist pointing out the even bigger baby who might need a nap, too. Of course I should have known that this would turn into an issue, especially with Cosmas, who had no interest in being social and never understood the whole concept of "sharing." He was a guy who worked all the time, and the time that he didn't spend at work, he wanted to sleep, and the time that was left over, he wanted to spend with me (lucky me, huh?), and he wasn't used to having my attention diverted to another man, er, male, whether it be bipedal, or otherwise. But I saw no sense in having to discuss this all now, so I just sucked it up for the moment and apologized. "I'm sorry I didn't pay attention to you earlier. Bad wife. Bad. Bad."

This got me no response, probably due to the fact that I was still alluding to the dog, however obliquely . . . and, of course, innocently.

It was then that I took another tack and tried to pry out the legal pad from his hands, but he wasn't about to let me off that easily.

"Please," I said.

Begrudgingly he turned over and faced me, and I continued, "C'mon. Please please tell me about Plan A, B, and C. I'm dying to hear." I then started giving him a back scratch, which I knew would seal the deal.

It was then that I found out that LOTR was an abbreviation for *The Lord of the Rings* (crazy that I hadn't cracked that one on my own, right?), which probably ranked only slightly lower than *The Matrix* sequels in his world and certainly well over most everything else (including things like food, water, and shelter), and to be fair I must explain that where in normal households the opening of a movie was something that was casually discussed along the lines of "Oh, *The Lord of the Rings* is opening this week, maybe we should go?" in our household it was anything but casual. Movies in our household were a very big deal—basically, a silent clause in our marital vows, sandwiched between "for richer or poorer" and "in sickness and health" was "through chick flicks and action-adventure sequels. . . ." In *our* household, *Blade 2* was celebrated by cutting out the full-page *New York Times* ad and sticking it on our front door with countdown days to the big event, and *The Lord of the Rings* was a much bigger deal—like huge. Tantamount in our household to the popularity of the Beatles in the '60s, a '70s Super Bowl between the Cowboys and the Steelers, big hair and big shoulder pads in the '80s, Princess Di in the '90s, and cargo pants in the new millennium.

LOTR was so big, in fact, that it deserved three different action plans—now we come back to Cosmas's charts—addressing everything from (1) how we wanted to secure tickets; to (2) what theater we would see it in; to (3) what time of day; to (4) whether we would have dinner before or after; and the all-important question of (5) where we would have dinner. (Cosmas viewed a good meal as inextricably linked to the pleasure of a good movie, and something of a backup, should the movie happen to be bad.)

I would have never forgotten such an important day in my husband's life, but with the arrival of the puppy I just hadn't been my usual self. Loath to admit this, I made a good show of carefully scrutinizing all three plans, including the restaurant choices and the movie-snack short list on page 2 (yes, there was a page 2). It was only after a few minutes of discussing the finer points of Italian versus Japanese when it came to hobbits and wizards that I began to take a good look at the movie times he had written down, and I remembered that the movie was three hours long . . . which didn't even take into account the fact we would have to wait in line for an hour to get good seats, and that the dinner would tack on at least another ninety minutes—all said, the whole thing was going to run a good three hours longer than our puppy's bladder.

Tired as I had become, I was unable to stop the anxiety spreading over my face, and Cosmas realized that something was dreadfully wrong.

"What? Are you mad that I figured out the plans on my own? Look, we can make up a Plan D together if you want to." So cute, so earnest, such big brown eyes—which of course made me think of the sleeping pup, which made me sneak a glance backward to check that someone hadn't broken in without our knowing and stolen away his crate in the last ten minutes.

That was it; that was the last straw. Cosmas immediately pulled away from me and sat up, which meant that things were about to get ugly, as I didn't ever recall him bailing on a back scratch.

I tried to beat him to the punch by speaking first. "You know that I love seeing movies, and of course I'm dying to see *The Lord of the Rings*, too, but, Cosmas, the movie is three hours long and you know we can't leave the puppy for that long. Maybe you should go by yourself."

As soon as it was out of my mouth, I regretted it but it was too late; the damage was done. The only thing worse than not being able to go see the movie on opening day was that I would dare suggest he see it alone.

I backtracked immediately. "I didn't mean that, you know I want to go with you. It's just that . . . that . . ."

But then the bellowing began. "I CAN'T BELIEVE YOU WOULD SUGGEST THAT I GO ALONE. HOW COULD I GO ALONE? WHOSE HAND WOULD I HOLD? WHO'S GOING TO SAVE THE SEATS WHEN ONE OF US IS AT THE CONCESSION STAND [that would be me; the deal was that he would wait in line for 95 percent of the movies, but for the really big movies, the ones that have marquee acronyms and require actual action plans, that was my job], WHO'S GOING TO FILL ME IN ON WHAT I MISS WHEN I GO TO THE BATHROOM?!"

There was really no good way to handle Cosmas once he'd begun to wig out, so I knew I just had to let it run its course, trying to interject with a bit of damage control here and there, all the while knowing perfectly well that he couldn't hear and puff out his eyeballs at the same time.

"I didn't mean that I didn't *want* to go with you. . . . Of course I'm dying to see the movie, too. . . . It's just that I know how important it is for you to see it on the opening day, and since I can't go because of . . ." I hesitated, not wanting to even go there. ". . . and so what I was saying is that perhaps you should go alone and I'll stay behind with . . . with . . ."— damn, we really needed to name the dog—"and of course I'm sure that his bladder issues will soon be resolved and then I'll go again with you. . . ." (The fact that Cosmas would end up sitting through the movie at least twice was a given.)

"It's not the same," he interrupted. "It's not how it used to be. Why can't things be like they were before . . . before . . ."

Well, that's it; I was officially starring in a Nickelodeon movie in which I was the only grown-up. Now my mind was in overdrive, as I knew that it was only a matter of time before the pup woke up and sauntered out of his crate, which would mean that he'd immediately need to go outside, which meant that I'd have to interrupt this joyous after-school special about jealousy and change. I was at the crossroads where I could either try to divert Cosmas's attention away from the obvious, or I could simply handle the problem head on, right this second, with patience, understanding, and some tough-ass love.

As I hadn't showered in days I figured that it might not be

too easy to seduce away his anger, so the first option was out, and it was a crapshoot whether the patience and understanding would even matter, since we *were* talking about LOTR. Damn those furry-footed little troublemakers . . . and then whammo, I had one of those divine inspirations that could only be attributed to sheer genius—either that or my lack of sleep had just pushed me over the sane edge into stupid.

"Cosmas, you know the story of *The Lord of the Rings*, right?"

His back still to me, he let out a big put-upon sigh, implying that, duh, *of course* he knew the story.

"So here's this group of guys who now have to travel far and wide so they can destroy the ring. . . ."

"It *wasn't* a group of guys. . . ."

"Okay, you're right. It *wasn't* a group of guys; in fact it was two men, a wizard, a dwarf, an elf, and three hobbits, okay?"

"Four." He turned to face me. Apparently, I was getting somewhere.

"Fine. Yes, four hobbits. And together they formed . . ."— I waved my hands, egging him on—"c'mon, what did they form?"

"A fellowship, obviously . . ."

"RIGHT! But don't you see? That's exactly what we're doing, right here, right now." I could tell by his puzzled look that I lost him with this; science guys can be so damn literal at times.

"Really, it's the same thing. We're all different species: me, you, and the pup."

"Um, even though I do wonder sometimes, but the last time I checked, you and I were actually the *same* species. . . ."

"COSMAS." I gave him a warning look; he nodded, and so I calmly continued, "So you're like the science-guy dwarf, and I'm the—"

"I'm not a dwarf!"

I took a deep breath. "Okay, so you're the science-guy elf"—I looked over and he seemed much more receptive to this—"and I'm the English major. . . ." I paused, as I didn't really want to be a dwarf, either, but if I said I was a man then that would only generate further debate given the fact that there were no chicks in the fellowship. Gritting my teeth, I continued. "So, I'm the incredibly svelte and stylish English-major dwarf, and our new puppy is the hobbit. And since hobbits are small and not the best fighters they need a great deal of protection from the others, right? And even though we're all so different [more than I'd ever known, I was beginning to see . . .] we have to put our differences behind us and come together to form a . . ."

"Fellowship?" Cosmas smiled.

I of course had planned on using the word *family*, but hey, you have to start somewhere. So then I continued explaining that since our little hobbit had particular limitations and couldn't be left on his own, the rest of us had to understand that everyone had limitations, and God help me, but I even quoted the preview where Cate Blanchett was talking to the hobbit and said, "Even the littlest hobbit could change the course of the world."

Now fully on board, Cosmas offered that perhaps this was similar to the part in the book when Frodo was stabbed by the ring-wraith and got sick, so that they all had to wait in the elfin kingdom until his evil wounds healed up. I agreed wholeheartedly—and with a certain amount of relief. Perhaps Cosmas now had a better understanding of how things would have to work from this point on. Any such hope was dashed, however, when Cosmas sighed and said, "It's just that everything was so great before and . . ." He stopped in mid-sentence and both of us watched as our four-legged hobbit emerged from his crate, and did the cutest little stretch and then wobbled a bit on the way back up, toppled over, and sat down hard on the floor.

It was then that I told Cosmas that, yes, things were indeed so great before when it was just the two of us, but that people change, and life goes on (okay, so I resort to clichés when tired). I explained that never in a million years would I ever have thought that I'd be a woman who actually owned a fanny pack (it's the one thing I've found where I can carry all my doggy supplies), as I knew it was a slippery slope from that to a minivan. Just as I had never thought I'd be caught dead on the street wearing sneakers and dirty sweatshirts. But situations changed, and I loved having a puppy and so the style sacrifice was more than worth it (although for the record, I don't actually *wear* the fanny pack around my waist; I sling it jauntily over my shoulder).

What it all came down to, I explained, in the fight against evil was that you had to learn to adapt to any situation, whether it be a band of angry orcs on the attack, or the awful fact of having to miss a movie on opening night.

Cosmas stopped in his tracks right then and said that there was one more thing—and since we were laying it all out on the table he wanted to get it off his chest.

I braced myself and followed him into the kitchen.

"I can't stand the fact that there are little baggies everywhere. I mean, what are they for, anyway?" He grabbed a few crumpled baggies that had been left on the kitchen table and waved them at me.

It took me a moment to realize that he wasn't joking, and that he actually had no idea what the baggies were for, which meant that it might be possible that he had no idea that you had to pick up a puppy's poo in an urban environment, which meant that he was in for a rude awakening.

In one quick motion I scooped up the hobbit, put my arm around my elf, gave my best dwarfish snortlike laugh . . . and said, "Boy, oh boy, do I have a mission for you." And with that, I prepared to initiate my husband into the fellowship.

The 10 Breeds of Obsessed Dog Owners

1. The Know-It-All Owner

This is the dog owner who claims to know every single thing about every single dog on the whole planet, and above all, *your* dog. Yes, it's true; they know the best food, the best training methods, and the best ways to discipline your pet. So much do they like to give advice, they will actually cross the street so they can walk right up to you and inform you that your dog is looking fat, and that obesity is the number-one health problem for dogs. They will then proceed to tell you that he might benefit from a little more exercise (of course they know the best agility school in the area) and that while giving treats is a sign of affection, so is taking your dog out for a brisk walk. Should you insist on feeding your dog to death then they'd be happy to recommend "a few low-fat treats that are really quite tasty." They start off most of their sentences with "Did you know?" and "Granted I'm just one person, but believe you me . . ." (What does that mean anyway, "believe you me"? Who talks like that? Also, I'd like to point out that Wendell is NOT plump, it's just the way his hair falls that makes him look a little broad—he's stocky, which is exactly how his breed should be.)

2

Do You Name Each of Your Dog's Toys?

THE YOUNG AND THE SQUEAKY

When I look back to the moments leading up to the squeaky ball's untimely demise, I guess I should have seen it coming. Cosmas was in a not-so-great mood after a sucky day at the lab; he had a headache; and he knew he was in charge of the dishes that night since I'd cooked dinner—though he begged off doing them until he was able to "calm his nerves" with a little bit of TV (which basically meant I would be stuck doing them the next morning). So there he was, trying to watch his new favorite show, *Alias* (sexy short-skirt-wearing secret agent—enough said), while Wendell happened to be cavorting around with his favorite toy, a little squeaky ball that we'd named, with perfect accuracy, the Most Annoying Toy in the World.

Now, the reason that this particular toy had been so named was that, whereas most other squeaky toys only squeaked when a dog bit into the toy and air rushed *out* of the squeaker doodad mechanism (hey, I'm no engineer), this toy also squeaked when air rushed back *into* the toy. In layman's terms, it squeaked all the damn time.

Cosmas asked nicely whether Wendell might play in the *other* room with the Most Annoying Toy in the World, and I tried several times to corral Wendell into the kitchen. But of course he wanted to be near us, and would eventually trot right back into the living room each time to resume play directly in front of the TV. I couldn't help noticing Cosmas's grip stiffen on the remote, and decided it was probably in everyone's best interest that I take the ball away from Wendell and put it back into his blue plastic bone-shaped toy chest—hoping that the laws of "out of sight, out of mind" would soon kick in. No such luck. Wendell just mooned away for his ball, walking in circles, whining and sniffing around for it here and there (this I don't quite get, as he'd *seen* where I put the damn thing away) before finally sitting smack in front of us on the couch and giving us a few little woofs that said, "Hey, no fair. Gimme back my ball."

This continued for ten minutes, and at the next commercial break Cosmas leapt to his feet, strode into the kitchen, and grabbed the ball out of the toy chest—which of course threw Wendell into a tizzy, as the only thing better than playing with his ball alone was having someone to play ball *with* him. Needless to say, however, Cosmas was not exactly in "play mode." Scanning the kitchen for a moment, he grabbed something off the counter, and then, in a scene straight out of a horror flick, raised what appeared to be a black Bic pen over his head . . . and stabbed it down into the squeaker hole of the ball—once, with feeling, then twice, sharply, and then, on the third downward plunge, simply leaving the pen where it was, plunged into the now mutilated squeak-hole. With my own private Bernard Herrmann score ripping through my head, I leapt to my feet and began frantically trying to pin Cosmas's arms to his sides from behind, shouting, "WHAT THE HELL ARE YOU DOING? HAVE YOU LOST YOUR FREAKIN' MIND?!"

Cosmas froze where he stood, as did Wendell, and we all stared uncomprehendingly at the little ball and the black Bic pen now sticking brutally out of it. It wasn't pretty—sort of *Friday the 13th* meets *Toy Story*. Eventually I let Cosmas's arms go and reached for the ball, careful to block Wendell's view. I pulled the pen out, half expecting the Most Annoying Toy in the World to go completely limp in my hands. But somehow Cosmas had not actually punctured the ball itself—merely the squeaker hole at its core. I took a deep breath, working up the nerve to do whatever needed to be done, and then shut my eyes as I hazarded a squeeze. . . . It was official. Cosmas had killed it.

Now when you squeezed the ball, all you heard was a sad little *phhsssst* noise when you pressed it, and then as the air started rushing back, you heard an even less inspiring *sssssssssssp* (perhaps we now needed to rename this the Most Deeply Depressed Ball in the World).

Finally finding words, Cosmas spoke very quietly. "I was just trying to get it to stop making that noise."

I sighed, thinking to myself, *Yeah, right, and those savage little boys on that island were just playing hide and seek with a pig.* "Well, what can I say?" I replied. "Success."

Rolling his eyes at my half-inflated sarcasm, he took the ball out of my hands and, after studying it for a moment, said he was pretty sure Wendell would still like it. He bent down and showed it to Wendell, who barked an "It's about time" at him, and then tossed it across the living room. Wendell went racing after it like always. But just as he pounced on it, grabbing it in his mouth and biting down, I couldn't help flinching.

Phhsssssssstttt.

Wendell dropped the ball, and the air began to suck back in halfheartedly, *sssssssssssssp.* He stared at it for a second and then pounced on it a second time. *Phhsssssssssstt.* He dropped the ball again and, before it could even begin to make another sad sound, walked back into the kitchen and sat before us as if to say, "Okay, enough with the lame decoy, where's the real thing?" He blinked up at us, and we blinked back down at him. No one spoke. This was when he lay down and put his head between his paws.

"OH MY GOD, HE'S HEARTBROKEN," I cried. "YOU KILLED HIS BALL. I CAN'T BELIEVE IT. THAT WAS HIS FAVORITE TOY! I CAN'T EVEN GET ANOTHER ONE BECAUSE I GOT IT IN

TENNESSEE WHEN WE WERE THERE FOR CHRISTMAS!"

I knew Cosmas felt bad, and wasn't sure whether I should just let it go or proceed to make him feel even worse. . . . I decided to go with the latter, angry at the thought that I no longer had a sure-fire way to keep Wendell busy for the odd half hour or forty minutes when I needed peace and freedom. And it wasn't as if *Cosmas* was the one who was home all day with him. I mean, how selfish could you get?!

"DO YOU HAVE ANY IDEA HOW MANY TOYS WE'VE GONE THROUGH IN ORDER TO FIND ONE THAT HE LOVES?" I shouted.

Cosmas said he was sorry, and I told him it wasn't *me* he should be apologizing to. Before I could finish that thought, I found myself marching across the room to find the ball, which a moment later I placed into Cosmas's hands, telling him that on second thought I didn't want him to apologize to Wendell . . . I had something altogether different in mind.

Two little words, spoken very clearly. "FIX IT."

Cosmas gave me a quizzical look.

I then walked over to the hall closet, reached inside, and pulled out a plastic bag, which I handed to him. Cosmas opened the bag and peered inside at the jumble of reject toys Wendell hadn't seemed to care for, but which I couldn't quite bring myself to throw away. (Was there no Salvation Army organization to take used dog toys?) Cosmas shook his head, still unable to follow where I was going with this.

Exasperated, I reached into the bag, pulled out a little

terry-cloth bear that was named Barney, and gave it a squeeze. Sure enough, Barney squeaked. Cosmas leaned forward, scrunching up his face, and stared really hard at Barney, as if half expecting the stuffed bear to spell it out for him. So I explained that, as the majority of these toys happened to be of a squeaky nature, and as he was a doctor, I wanted him to perform a squeakendectomy. Basically to take the squeaker out of one of *these* toys and then put it in the ball—a squeaker-transplant procedure, if you will. Now granted, Cosmas was a gastroenterologist who preferred research to patient care and hadn't done surgery since med school, but so what, hadn't he taken the Hippocratic oath swearing to help anyone who needed it?

He started to laugh, but only got halfway through his third set of *ha-has* before suddenly taking in my scowl and the hands I had placed squarely on my hips. "I'm completely serious," I said. He asked why we couldn't just buy another ball, and I told him that *he* certainly could, but that in that case he'd have to book a standby flight to Tennessee to do so, because duh, it's not as if I haven't been on the lookout for another one just like it in our greater metropolitan area (as a spare, of course—I may have despised the thing, after all, but I was a nice mom). This gave Cosmas a moment's pause, as he knew I wasn't exaggerating. If ever there was a heat-seeking-missile-of-a-shopper, it was me.

In a last-ditch stroll through the valley of denial (that his night of watching-TV-while-shirking-the-dishes was now, apparently, over), Cosmas bent down to show Wendell the

ball again. Wendell immediately lifted his head, but this time
I swear there was a different sort of look in his eyes—as if he
wasn't sure he could handle being teased like this. Cosmas
squatted down and rolled the ball toward Wendell's nose.
Halfheartedly, Wendell took it in his mouth, bit into it
(*phhsssssssssstt*), and then promptly dropped it (*ssssssssssssp*),
watching it roll away even as he put his head back between
his paws.

Soon the kitchen table was wiped clean, and all the supplies were gathered—our sharpest paring knife, superglue,
duct tape, tweezers, Scotch tape, desk lamp, Mini Maglite
flashlight, all the hotel sewing kits I could find, and scissors.
I will say that those ER doctors on TV have *nothing* on
Cosmas, because as soon as we'd assembled the necessary
supplies, he was all business. You know, not one extraneous
movement, brisk and intense to the last. I was his trusted as-
sistant, and did whatever was required—holding the flashlight, handing him the tools, and even once wiping a little
bead of sweat off his brow (just like in the movies!).

Pretty soon there was stuffing fluff littered all over the
table, and Barney lay by the wayside, disemboweled. Cosmas
had carefully made an L-shaped incision in the ball, pulled
back the flap, and peered inside it, trying to figure out the in-
tricacies of its anatomy. While he studied, he instructed me
to gather up the fluff, restuff Barney as best I could (perhaps
adding in a few cotton balls where the squeaker once lay), and
then sew him up. In a normal situation, I would have found
this request absurd, because Barney was pretty much headed

for the nearest landfill anyway, but somehow on this particular night, it seemed like the right thing to do.

Once Barney was resting on a pillow, comfortably in recovery, I asked Cosmas how the real "patient" was doing. He shook his head and said this might not be as straightforward as it had at first seemed. Hmmm, this didn't sound good. It seemed that this particular ball's squeaker (an inner core that worked with tubing and a pinhole on the outside of the toy) was totally different from the one found in your basic animal toy, like Barney, for instance (who simply featured a little plastic pouch that was a self-contained squeaker). Cosmas muttered something about "testing for 'organ compatibility' beforehand. . . ."

An hour later, we had another three toys in recovery alongside Barney, and Cosmas was in the process of "closing up." In the end, Cosmas had actually stuffed three different squeaker pouches into the gut of the ball, in hopes that a sufficient amount of squeak power might be thereby produced. The best thing to close up with, of course, was Krazy Glue, but I quickly raised the fact that as Wendell would have this thing in his mouth, something as toxic (and misspelled) as Krazy Glue might not be a great idea. The last thing we needed was to have the Most Annoying Toy in the World end up actually killing the dog who loved it. But we didn't have the right needle and thread, and that would have just left air holes anyway. So Cosmas resolved to use the glue after all, but with carefully cut strips of duct tape placed over the glued areas for protection.

It was now late, and Cosmas said we had to let the glue dry and wouldn't know the outcome until morning. When I asked for a prognosis, Cosmas told me that, due to unknown variables (the glue, the internal damage that he couldn't repair from the pen wounds, and the inexact squeaker match), the best he could give the Most Annoying Toy in the World was fifty-fifty. Carefully I placed it on the recovery pillow next to the other toys, and Cosmas and I got ready for bed. It was now close to two in the morning.

A few minutes later, lying in the dark with Wendell at our feet, Cosmas told me he felt really bad about the whole thing. I assured him that if it hadn't been him, it probably would have been me, as I, too, had harbored fantasies of the ball's mysterious disappearance (though I can't say I'd ever have done the job quite so violently . . .). Cosmas laughed. And I told him that he'd more than made up for everything by spending the last few hours slaving away in toy surgery. No matter what happened in the morning, we both knew he'd done everything he could.

Just then Wendell did that thing where he rolls over onto his back with his front paws straight up in the air while totally asleep, and we watched as his feet moved a bit, running in his dreams. Chasing rabbits, maybe? Or, more likely, running after the Most Annoying Toy in the World . . .*

Ah, the things you do for love.

---

* I am pleased to report that the Most Annoying Toy in the World did ultimately pull through (it was a little touch-and-go for a few days) and was back in action by the following week.

The Ten Commandments of Dog Obsession

Thou shalt not make fun of my dog. Ever.

Thou shalt not take my dog's name in vain (i.e., I can yell at my dog, but you can't).

Thou shalt not call my dog fat (i.e., I can say my dog is a little plump, but you can't).

Thou shalt not ever utter the words "He's *just* a dog."

Thou shalt not say my neighbor's dog is cuter.

Thou shalt never speak of dogs dying in front of my dog or in front of me when I have PMS and am feeling oversensitive.

Thou shalt not call into question the intelligence of my dog—trust me, on many levels he's smarter than you.

Thou shalt not say that my dog looks hungry in a way that implies that I am negligent when it comes to the feeding of my dog. Like I'd really ever forget to feed my dog. (Dogs are always hungry; it's what they do for a living.)

Thou shalt not say that my dog's breath smells bad, as most dogs' breath smells but they can't help it; please see commandment number one above.

Thou shalt not lie, cheat, or steal unless it's for the good of my dog, in which case it may very well be justified. 🐾

The 10 Breeds of
Obsessed Dog Owners

2. The Tofu Owner

This is the dog owner who loves not only dogs, but *all* creatures. They make a point of not only removing the ticks from their dog (careful not to rip their little heads off) but then actually release them back into the wild (where they can climb onto your dog and possibly infect him with disease). These dog owners practice yoga, eat vegetarian, and hate people who smoke (especially at the dog park). Not surprisingly, they are always a little cranky (probably due to an iron deficiency). They have taken it upon themselves to change thousands of years of evolutionary history, feeling certain that if dogs truly had a choice they would rather become friends with the small jackrabbit than devour it. Their dogs love tofu. Their dogs love broccoli. Cranky and a little too skinny, their dogs look as if they are constantly trying to figure out a way to ditch them to go beg outside a local McDonald's.

Do You Suspect Your Dog Is a Genius?

CROUCHING MOTHER, HIDDEN DRAGON

The whole idea of bitching and moaning about your mother, as all daughters bitch and moan about their mothers, and then one day suddenly realizing that you've *become* your mother is, of course, such a cliché. But if you stop to think what makes a cliché a cliché, it's the fact that, more often than not, things do just seem to happen that way.

Common Korean parental methodology has always held that in order to get your children into an Ivy League school they need to be well rounded. So not only were we Lee kids expected to perform at the top of the class when it came to academics, but we also had to play two sports *and* a musical instrument. And, not only did we have to play at least two sports and a musical instrument, but we also had to be good at them. Obviously when you're six years old, you don't tend to question such demands. Later on, though, when you get a bit older, bolder, and *freakin' sick of having to practice the violin every day for ninety freakin' minutes*, you start to question things from time to time.

So I would say, "Mom, why do I have to play the violin if I don't want to?" Her reply was always "Because I said so." Followed by a coy change in tone—"Don't you want to get into an Ivy League college?" Which would promptly lead into a discussion on why it was that I was *still* second chair in the St. Louis Youth Orchestra—you know, as opposed to first chair. In fact, it was this very topic that helped me truly master the art of rolling my eyes so well (very useful biofeedback, by the way).

Once, I decided to try the honest-but-may-be-seen-as-smart-alecky-approach-which-will-inevitably-lead-to-trouble: "Well, the reason I'm probably second chair is because Alison Taylor is just better than me." Now, nothing drove my mother more nuts than hearing things like that—first, because she was a mom (and all moms want to think their children are better than everyone else's); and secondly, because she was competitive as hell. Suddenly she'd start chopping whatever happened to be on the cutting board in front of her more aggressively (somehow I remember all of these conversations as taking place in the kitchen). Next she'd begin to mutter under her breath in Korean, which of course I couldn't understand. Finally, having brutalized the poor chicken at hand, or cut a cucumber into slices as razor-thin as optical lenses, she'd sigh, stop what she was doing, and then point me toward the chair at the kitchen table (this is where a good eye-roll could be particularly satisfying).

Lowering herself to the table, my mother would proceed to tell me the same thing she always told me—whether I'd just lost a tennis match, come in third in a swim meet, or received a mere 98 on the latest quiz; that the only reason she pushed me so hard was that she *knew* I could do it. She *knew* I had it in me to be first chair; she *knew* I had it in me to win the tennis match; she *knew* I had it in me to at least do a *little* better in swimming (I truly wasn't that good a swimmer, and she wasn't completely delusional).

Most of all, she *knew* I was more than smart enough to get not just straight A's, but straight A's derived from perfect scores on tests and the highest possible grade on every essay. At first I just took her words at face value, assuming that perhaps she *did* know that I could do all these things. Eventually, however, I began to question how she *knew* such things. But that only led me full circle to "Because I said so."

Anyway, fast-forward fifteen years . . .

It was the first day of puppy kindergarten. I was extremely nervous, but couldn't wait to show off all the tricks Wendell already knew at the tender age of sixteen weeks. I had read all the dog-training books and had been working with Wendell religiously (twice a day for twenty minutes) on "sit," "down," "shake," and "roll over."

Now imagine my self-satisfied glee when I found out that puppy kindergarten's main goal was merely to socialize our puppies so they might learn good manners from other dogs. Apparently there would only be a few basic commands that we would work on. Some puppies, the teacher explained, wouldn't have the concentration skills or discipline to do much more than "sit" and maybe "down" by the end of the seven-week course (ooooh, I thought, perhaps I should look into having Wendell skip kindergarten altogether!).

After letting all the dogs romp around together for most of the class, the teacher finally asked everyone to find a place on the floor and work with their dog on the command "sit." Quick on the uptake, I found a spot right in the center, whipped out the puppy biscuits I'd brought, and smiled down at Wendell appreciatively. "Sit," I said, already feeling the glow of achievement.

Wendell did *not* sit.

In fact, Wendell seemed not to have heard me at all, focused as he was on all the other dogs. He was straining so hard to reach the dogs nearest him, he could barely breathe. I was mortified, but luckily no one seemed to be paying any attention to us—well, no one except for the by-now very agitated man to my right whose shar-pei puppy Wendell was seriously provoking. I reeled Wendell in, squatted before him, waved a cookie in front of his nose, and voiced my command again: "Sit!"

Nothing.

I tried one more time, this time staring him straight in the eyes and using a tone that scared even me: "SIT."

Not one iota of recognition.

This was when the teacher tapped me on the shoulder lightly and said she'd like to see us both after class. Twenty-five mortifying minutes later, Wendell and I watched as everyone else filed out of the classroom. Or rather, I watched, while Wendell scratched desperately at the floor, straining so hard to follow them, he sounded like the love child of Brenda Vacarro and Darth Vader.

Now, I'm no sissy. In fact, at times I can be what Cosmas calls aggressively confident. But not that day. I was so intimidated, for some reason, that I thought I'd part my teeth and start panting hoarsely myself. Not in my entire life had I been asked to stay after class—I mean, not for something *bad.* . . .

Walking over to us, the teacher bent down to pet Wendell, who was wiggling his tail and jumping all about like a wild little animal that had just been leashed for the first time. After a moment's appraisal she turned and began to say something to me, and before I could even register what she was saying, I pinpointed the tone of voice: a heaping plateful of pity garnished with a sprig of sanctimony.

"Not all dogs are trainable," she said softly, nodding her head up and down slowly in that annoying (and illogical) way people always seem to when they're telling you something clearly *not* in the affirmative. Then she launched into terrier history—how they used to hunt vermin back in the day, and were very instinctual dogs with lots of energy, and blah, blah, blah—and that she'd known quite a few terriers who weren't so easily trained, so I shouldn't walk away from all of this thinking that my dog just wasn't very bright.

WHAT?!

Before she could go on, I interrupted her, explaining that she was totally mistaken—that in fact Wendell was *very* bright and *very* trainable. Then I informed her that Wendell already knew how to sit, as well as shake, lie down, and roll over.

She gave me one of those "whatever you need to say to make yourself feel better" nods (in the "affirmative," of course). And, I knew what she was thinking. She was thinking that in the ten years she'd probably been teaching puppy K, every class had yielded at least one crazy dog-mom who thought her dog was a genius when in fact he was, hands down, the dumbest one of the lot. Needless to say, this infuriated me. Oh, how I wished for a large cutting board, a carrot, and a really sharp knife, so I could work out my aggressions like a lady!

In desperation, I dug around in my pocket, pulled out a biscuit, and held it in front of my dog, saying, "Wendell, sit." But to no avail. Tuckered out from all the recent excitement, he merely lay on the ground panting, no matter how much ESP I tried.

The teacher reached over and took the treat out of my hand, examining it thoughtfully for a moment. "You know, you might want to get better treats," she said. "You'll probably find he responds better if you have something really good."

GOOD LORD! WHO *WAS* THIS WOMAN, KICKING ME WHEN I WAS DOWN? HOW DARE SHE IMPLY THAT I, THE WOMAN WHO DID *HOURS* OF RESEARCH ON THE INTERNET IN SEARCH OF THE MOST SCRUMPTIOUS YET HIGHLY NUTRITIOUS TREATS, WOULD SUB- JECT HER PUPPY—WHO, SPEAKING OF, WAS

FAR SMARTER THAN ALL THE OTHER WHINY LITTLE DOGS IN THE CLASS—TO INFERIOR TREATS?!!

I kept my voice (heroically) from shaking as I told her that normally Wendell adored these *highly nutritious* treats. That, really, he just gobbled them up at home. Again, I got the "poor, crazy you" nod. She then explained that at home, of course, Wendell might very well be attentive to me, because there was nothing else going on, whereas here at school there were all these other puppies to distract him, and perhaps if I brought, say, a hot dog or bologna to class next week, I might be able to get his attention. Okay, I was still pissed, but this sorta made sense to me, so I gave her a meek nod back to show acquiescence (look, I could play beta to her alpha, if that was her game . . .).

But apparently she wasn't finished yet. Wendell "obviously" had "control issues" (guess the lunging/choking/barking must have tipped her off). So I "might want to try out a pinch collar to see if that works a little better." Of course, normally she "wouldn't *recommend* using a pinch collar on a puppy so young," but somehow she felt that it might be "necessary in Wendell's case."

Never had I been so dejected and upset. By the time I picked up Cosmas from work, the mix of anger, worry, and hard-core indignation in my chest had rendered me almost completely mute. Stepping into the car, Cosmas took one look at my face and knew that puppy kindergarten had not gone well.

When we arrived home, I let Cosmas walk our by-now-very-tired-out puppy while I went upstairs to fume in our room alone. Later, in bed, I told him everything that had happened (through dwindling, half-dried tears), and that, though I couldn't explain *how* I knew—and though all evidence appeared to contradict it—I had this incredible certainty that Wendell was actually . . . a genius.

Knowing my ego wouldn't bear even the tiniest tap in its current condition, Cosmas allowed that, yes, he, too, had been thinking that Wendell seemed unusually smart. Though, of course, Cosmas had absolutely no frame of reference to base this on, since he'd never even *had* a dog before. Nonetheless, this must have satisfied me, because in just a few hours I was asleep.

As the weeks went on, I was vindicated, of course. I had taken the teacher's advice and brought better treats (you know, filet mignon seasoned with salt and garlic—hey, this girl doesn't mess around) and a pinch collar—both of which worked to prove that not only was Wendell very smart and basically well behaved, but also that he knew by far the most tricks of any dog there.

Even after kindergarten I continued with Wendell's rigorous training program, perfecting old tricks and slowly teaching him new ones. His latest were shaking hands, knowing how to switch to the other hand (he was ambidextrous), how to slap a high-five, and, of course, the crowning achievement, which was that when I pointed a finger gun at Wendell and said "bang-bang," he'd roll over onto his back, splay out his paws, and play dead. (He could even do it without the bang-bang, on just the signal of the "gun" being aimed at him.)

The trick I started to have problems with was "go stealth," which involved Wendell crawling on his belly sort of like Tom Cruise in *Mission: Impossible* (the plan was to incorporate the theme music later on). So I was talking to my older brother, John, about it one night and explaining that normally Wendell would do absolutely anything for a nacho cheese Dorito (like mother, like dog), but somehow even this wasn't enough incentive. . . .

That's when my brother began to quiz me ever so subtly about the number of tricks Wendell knew. Then he asked Wendell's age. Finally he asked me whether Wendell might not be a little young for so much training—after all, he was still only seven months old, and a lot of books indicated that you should wait as long as a year to teach specific tasks. Naturally I scoffed at this; Wendell was obviously the exception to the rule. Then, in a low voice, I revealed that I was currently looking into canine IQ tests, as I had strong suspicions Wendell might be a genius. . . .

John hesitated a moment, and then suggested that perhaps I was putting too much pressure on Wendell. I couldn't tell if he was just trying to be funny—you know, to aggravate me in that older-brother way—or whether he was actually serious. But I replied very matter-of-factly that I was not pressuring Wendell in the least. And, besides, even if I *was* pushing him to achieve certain things, then it was simply because I *knew* he could do it.

"And what, precisely, leads you to believe Wendell's capable of becoming Tom Cruise?" John asked.

Without a moment's hesitation I stepped right into the trap: *"Because I said so."*

Those four words seemed to echo through the room, and I literally clapped my hand over my mouth in horror, dropping the phone. OH, MY GOD—I had turned into my own mom. Worse yet, I had turned into my mom over a beginning obedience class and a few doggie tricks. I could just hear my brother's smugness on the other end of the line.

So he didn't have a chance to say a word before I picked the phone back up, told him to shove it, and then hung up.

That night, I spent a long time staring at Wendell, who was asleep in the little space between the bookshelf and the sofa. And I wondered how it had all happened. . . . Was this in my genes? Was it my fate? Was Wendell now feeling stressed out and pressured by all the drive and determination that I had truly believed were in his own best interests?

It grew late into the evening, and then finally, after much deliberation, I decided that maybe my mom *had* been right all those years about my being smart enough and capable enough to do all those things, well, if only I really tried. Maybe she *did* just know. . . .

Just as I now *knew*, too (a mother's intuition is very strong, of course). Wendell was capable of great things. He just needed a little friendly and constructive nudging on my part.

After all, he was Mommy's little genius.

How to Take Your Dog Out
for His Last Stroll of the Evening

Jerk awake suddenly, reflexively wiping the drool off your chin and checking to make sure that you didn't get any on the couch (if you did, quickly flip the couch cushion and try to remember to make sure that the zipper side is on the inside). Blink a few times rapidly and squint at your watch to see what time it is and then look out the window to make sure that it's still dark out and you haven't in fact just slept through the night and into the middle of the next day.

Hit the power button as you pass the TV and just before you turn off the light in the living room give a quick look behind you to see that your dog is asleep on his back in the little space between the couch and the bookshelf. Instead of feeling the normal feeling of love and warm fuzzies toward your darling sleeping dog, feel a pang of dismay as you realize that before you can go to bed you must walk your dog one more time. Too tired to roll your eyes at this idea, simply let out a little bit of your stale breath making a *pthhhhhh* sound to no one in particular.

Try to remember when the dog was last walked and wonder whether it might be nicer of you not to interrupt his sleep by dragging him out into the dark of night, even though he hasn't gone out in over five hours and you plan to sleep for at least another seven or eight hours.

Realizing that this is only a recipe for disaster, you walk over to your dog, rubbing his warm belly, and say, "C'mon, you . . . time to go outside." Watch your dog stretch out his legs and roll over to his side, completely ignoring you, and give him a little pat and say, "C'mon, buddy. I'm sleepy, too, but the sooner you get up, the sooner we get this over with."

Sigh loudly as he rolls over away from you and say in your best sleepy singsong voice, "Who wants to go outside? Daddy's going outside. Daddy is going outside and you have to stay. Be a good boy as Daddy goes bye-bye." Feel chagrined as this reverse-psychology trick fails miserably, but you continue the charade and walk toward the door, where you slip on your loafers and pointedly look for your keys.

Open the door and stomp your feet as if you are walking out and then close the door loudly even though you are still in your apartment but you know your dog cannot see the doorway with his eyes closed and his face turned away from you. Wait a few seconds to see if you hear anything. Nothing. Open the door again and close it so he thinks that you came back into the apartment (no need to get caught in a lie, right?) and then call out your dog's name in your best whiny, soulful voice. Nothing. Slap your thigh and simply say, "Come." Nothing. Say, "Now." Nothing.

Sigh again and then start walking back toward the living room, where you will see that your dog's eyes are open but he is not making any movement to get up. This is when you crouch down and attach his collar and then stand up and give it the tiniest of tugs to show that you mean business. Watch as your dog arches his back and gives the smallest little whimper as if you are hurting his neck even though you know you are not. Pull again and watch as you have now slid your dog a good two inches across the floor by his neck and still he is refusing to get up. Say, "Get up." Say, "Now." Feeling bad for being so gruff, say, "Please, Wendell. Please get up."

Groan as you realize how heavy your little dog has become as you try to lift him off the floor and move on to the next tactic, which is not to pick him up totally, but just pick him up enough so that he is forced to either stand or fall onto the floor. Watch with satisfaction as your dog realizes he has lost the battle and starts to walk behind you as you head toward the door. Try not to be annoyed as he stops at his water bowl to drink for a while even though you know he's not particularly thirsty (he's just saving face since you won the contest of wills [Hooray!]).

Once you're outside, your dog is now fully awake and happy to be there as there are lots of interesting smells and plenty of reasons to disturb your sleeping neighbors by barking. Start to yawn as you wait for the business at hand to be completed, and warn him that he'd better hurry. As he gets the hint, watch your dog do the little squat that basically says night-night for you both. Pat him on the head and say, "Good job."

Repeat every night for the rest of his life. 🐾

The 10 Breeds of
Obsessed Dog Owners

3. The Competitive Owner

This is the dog owner who thinks that their dog is better than your dog (and probably better than you too). Their dog can do no wrong. Their dog is perfect. Their dog can walk off leash. Their dog is one step away from walking upright, growing thumbs, and would probably win the Nobel prize if there happened to be a category in which dogs could be nominated. No matter how smart your dog is, their dog is smarter. No matter how many tricks your dog knows, their dog knows more (though they may not feel like doing a one-off competition right this second, being independent and immune to the bullying or persuasion that might impress a lesser specimen). This owner literally thinks that their dog's poop doesn't stink. "No really, it's sort of amazing, but it doesn't seem to have an odor at all, well, maybe a little, but kind of reminiscent of a freshly turned field before planting." This is when you should say that according to your gastroenterologist husband, all poop stinks and in fact, in judging poop, the stinkier, the better. (Full disclosure: My husband tells me this isn't actually true, but I don't care; it sounds good.)

4

Is Money No Object
When It Comes to Your Dog?

DOG, LIES, AND VIDEOTAPE

I call my husband, Cosmas, from the Best Buy digital video camera section. He answers on the first ring, but he doesn't say hello. This is something he does when he's really consumed by work (genetics, biology, genes, blue yeast . . . don't ask). So picking up the phone is an involuntary reaction that he just does, not remembering that he's supposed to actually say hello. But I know the drill, so I say, "Hello, hello, earth to space lab, come in, come in." (Or if I'm in a bitchy mood, I just say, "Hello. Hello. Hello," over and over again until the annoying point where he says, "What?")

But since I want something I need to keep it all friendly, so I patiently wait until he stops typing on his computer (though I'm pretty sure he'll now use this "commercial" break to check his E-mail). "What's up, sweetie?"

"Busy today?"

"Mmm." (This means yes.)

"Well, I'll be quick. So I'm in Best Buy and I'm thinking we need a digital video camera." I try to keep my voice very casual and light, as if I'm letting him know I'm about to buy a pack of gum.

I hold my breath, hoping that his overworked brain will finally favor me for a change, by having him mumble something along the lines of sure, whatever you want, just to get me off the phone.

I hear him typing again, obviously responding to E-mail now. I clear my throat—cliché move, but it works. "Hmmm, what? Can we talk about this tonight when you get home?"

Now I'm testy, as I have actually been in Manhattan for the past two days and won't even be returning to our home in Boston for at least another two days (though probably now three, since he obviously hasn't noticed my absence).

"Cosmas, I'm in New York, remember?"

"Right. Oh God, what time is it? Do I need to go walk Wendell?" (At least Cosmas tries his best to be good doggie daddy and normally remembers that dogs need to be walked on a regular basis, though getting him to remember to walk him *and* feed him is the next goal.)

I can't hold back my sigh. "Wendell is with me." I refrain from asking him whether he's been actually going home at lunchtime to walk him, which I'm willing to bet he has.

"That's right. Yes, he wasn't home today at lunchtime." (You would think that coming home to walk your dog only to find that he's nowhere to be found would cause panic in most people, and it probably did with Cosmas, but then he must have gotten distracted by, say, trying to remember where he put the peanut butter, and then forgotten all about it—twenty minutes later he'd have jelly at the sides of his mouth and he'd be whistling his way off to work.)

My normal response to all of this would be to get my screechy voice on and give him a lecture, but because I'm in my beloved New York, I find that I don't care as much. So I decide to just give in to my New Yorker inclinations (I had only moved away to Cambridge two years ago, so it's not like I've lost my touch), which is to hang up on him and just buy the camera.

Ten minutes later as I'm standing in line still trying to convince myself that a silver matte finish really isn't worth an extra hundred bucks, my phone begins to ring. I don't hear it, but Wendell does and whines a little, as he has a weird aversion to electronic beeps (the only time I get spacey is when charging large amounts of money). I look at the little picture of an office building that appears on my phone screen next to the flashing word *husband*. Reluctantly, I pick up. "Best Buy Video-Camera Department?"

He pauses and then says, "Uhm, yes, I'm looking for my wife. I think she's in your department. She's five four, dark hair, and weighs about . . ."

"Cosmas! It's me," I yell into the phone, stopping him from breaking one of the Ten Commandments: Thou shalt never utter thy wife's estimated weight over an unsecured phone line.

"You're in line already, aren't you?"

I was going to lie, but it's easier to be brave when you're four hundred miles away. "Yep. Look, our moment to discuss this is over, okay? You had your chance, but obviously an all-important work E-mail got in the way of something as insignificant as your wife. I mean, God, forget my feelings, think about Wendell. He's just a baby." I always get a little more melodramatic when I know someone is listening to my conversation (I grew up watching *Dynasty* and *Dallas*), as I am now at the front of the line and standing in front of a register woman named Marlene, who gives me the "you tell it to him straight, sister" nod of approval. I give her a thumbs-up sign and step to the side, indicating that she should take the next customer.

"Why do we need a video camera?"

I take a deep breath and whisper into the phone, "I want to record Wendell's swimming lesson."

I decide to continue, because even I'm aware that a swimming lesson for a dog probably needs a bit further explanation. "Look, I found this place called Bonnie's K9 Corp, it's actually for pet hydrotherapy, but they also host swim play groups for dogs, too, and I thought that would be fun for Wendell, especially since it's going to rain tomorrow so I can't take him to the dog run, but when I registered him for the swim group, I got to talking with the owner about the fact that Wendell actually seems afraid of the water, and even though it's obvious that Wendell could probably swim, I thought perhaps it wouldn't be a bad idea to get him one lesson to make sure. I mean, good god, you know that most New Englanders have retrievers and Labs and if he's going to be able to play, he's got to make up for his smaller size by really being a strong swimmer. I mean, it's not like there are lifeguards for dogs."

Now it's Cosmas's turn to sigh. After three years of marriage, he is now wise enough to know which battles he can win (like the fact that we don't really need to spend eight hundred dollars on a video camera, especially when I know nothing about them and am obviously just defaulting to the laws of female technology-buying behavior—when in doubt, buy the most expensive one with the most features, and the smallest model you can afford). The battles that he now knows he shouldn't even bother with are the ones that are just totally outrageously outlandish, like say, a private swimming lesson for our dog.

"Think of Wendell's photo album."

I say, "What?" but I know exactly what he is doing. He is making a not so subtle point to say that for the first time in my life I had put together a photo album (our honeymoon pictures didn't even make the cut and were relegated to a shoebox underneath our bed) containing Wendell's entire life—from the day we got him I've been photographing everything: his first snow, his first bath, his first bone, his first rawhide, his first Halloween (he went berserk when I stuffed him into a pumpkin costume, so he was an angel instead), his first car trip, his first time in New York City, his first time at the beach. . . . So what he is saying is that if I switch mediums from still photos to video then I won't be able to complete the magnum opus album of his life (the photo album is actually called "The Magnum Opus of Wendell: A Symphony of Pictures").

"You know, I think the model I'm buying actually takes stills, too." Ha, smear that on a slide and stuff it in your microscope, science boy.

He is quiet for so long that I wonder whether I had accidentally said my "science-boy" comment out loud. Oops. "A video camera is not something that should be purchased on a whim. I promise I'll look into them. I mean, what happens if you get one, and the new models come out next month?"

Now, this is a viable point, because nothing makes me madder than caving in to the peer pressure of the latest, greatest cell phone, only to have a newer, smaller, cuter, sleeker model come out a month later.

He knows I'm coming around because I'm not responding, and dead air is a rarity for me. "And, besides, do you really want to be stuck behind a camera for Wendell's first swimming lesson? It's so cold, so aloof, so Oliver Stone."

The deciding factor is that Wendell has now decided that he has been a "good shopping boy" for quite long enough, and is now tugging at the leash. I love the way he becomes a four-legged New Yorker whenever we are in the city, so attuned to the fact that if you want something in this town, then you'd better speak up. On cue, Wendell woofs, just one short bark to say, "Enough." "Let's go." "Now." "Let's go find a Mr. Softee and get a cherry-dip cone!"

With Wendell leading the way out of the store, I actually feel somewhat relieved by the fact that I am letting the whole video-camera thing go—because it's not like I have time to figure out how to work the thing when I have dinner and drinks dates set up for this evening, and Wendell's lesson is first thing in the morning (so the instructor will be sharp, and the pool will be clean). Besides, the whole video thing might be a little too suburban soccer mom for me, and even though only a New Yorker would actually even book her dog for a private swim lesson (this being that it was probably only in Manhattan that dog swimming pools even existed), I bet New Yorkers don't even really film their kids, they probably hire people to do it for them. My last thought right before I spot a Mr. Softee truck three blocks down, across the street, almost blocked by a FedEx truck, is whether Oliver Stone might be available for a last-minute gig.

🐾   🐾   🐾

Wendell was cranky on the morning of his first swim lesson, probably due to the fact that he knew the Union Square dog run was in the opposite direction from where we were headed. While getting ready in the morning I had debated taking him to the dog run first, but then had decided against it, thinking that it might not be best to have him all tired out beforehand. His displeasure might also have been due to the fact that I had chintzed out on his normal breakfast portion to ensure that he had more than enough time for proper digestion before he hit the water (everyone knows that a leg cramp can be fatal in even the shallowest of waters).

On the way over to Ninth Avenue I stopped in a deli to buy more film, but found myself a bit perplexed as I tried to make sense of all the picture symbols on the back of the packaging. The pool was indoors, so I didn't need to bother with the sun symbol, but it wasn't clear which was the best speed for action photos. I asked a woman with a stroller her opinion and she told me that the 200-speed film had been suitable when her baby had started to crawl. I nodded at this and explained that it was Wendell's first swimming lesson, and I was pretty sure that even though wheaten terriers weren't famous for their swimming prowess, I was pretty sure that Wendell could easily trump her baby's fastest time across their kitchen floor. (What can I say, we New Yorkers are a competitive bunch.) I bought one of each speed and decided that I could probably make it through three rolls if necessary because I could always extend the half-hour lesson to an hour if needed.

Wendell perked up as soon as we got to Bonnie's K9 Corp, because there were at least four other dogs running about the office. Once I checked the sturdiness of the security fence that was blocking the access to the pool, I let him off leash to romp around with the other dogs. I handed the receptionist all of Wendell's signed forms, and tried to calm my nerves by reading the framed write-ups hanging on the walls. They had been featured in *Town & Country*, which I felt was a good sign, as surely the magazine's legal department would have researched any cases of accidental-drowning incidents or pending lawsuits before publishing a feature story.

I felt immediately better when I met Marge, the teacher, who was a very strong-looking woman in a wet suit. She explained that she normally did the hydrotherapy sessions, and that she worked with dogs that were well over 150 pounds, some of whom had such bad arthritis in their legs that they wouldn't be able to make it out of the pool without her help. Yes, it was obvious that she could probably do one-armed curls with Wendell's forty-pound frame if she so desired.

For the first five minutes she let Wendell get used to his surroundings, which he did by running around and around the perimeter of the pool barking at the two large German shepherds that were happily paddling about and bobbing around at the floating tennis balls. While I was waiting I had purchased Wendell a darling little orange fishy floating toy, sort of as a souvenir, and I asked Marge whether she wanted to use it to entice him into the water. When I pulled the toy out of my purse, Wendell was immediately by my side (like mother, like dog when it came to new baubles). I waved the toy in front of his face, and he immediately lay down before me. I then tossed the toy to Marge, which of course caused Wendell to leap up so that he could charge Marge, but before he even made it to her she tossed it right into the pool. Without a moment's hesitation, Wendell jumped for it and did what can only be described as the doggie version of a belly flop, landing smack in the middle of the pool.

Honestly, the whole thing happened so fast, it was a toss-up as to whether Wendell or I was the most surprised, but surprised when mixed with water quickly turned into fear as

Wendell started to flail about frantically, obviously unable to get a footing in the three-foot-deep water. His eyes were wild, but I think my own were wilder as I tossed my camera toward the chair, kicked off my shoes, and was at the edge, ready to jump in to save him. As I teetered on the edge, arms moving in wild circles to maintain balance, Marge had quickly slid into the water and was by Wendell's side. By this time Wendell's canine instincts had kicked in and he was furiously dog-paddling toward the steps. A moment later and he was out of the pool, dripping wet, mad as hell, and barking like crazy.

I must say I was more than a little taken aback about this method of introducing a dog to water, which seemed only one step less beastly than those stories of farm kids whose parents taught them to swim by throwing them in the local watering hole (talk about a splashy start to a lifetime of extended therapy). Now, maybe Marge was raised in the backwoods of Montana, but she was a long way from home and I was ready to tell her that things worked differently here in the city.

Marge must have sensed my uneasiness (perhaps my clenched fists, grim expression, and the way I was poised to dial 911 on my cell phone gave it away) and told me that Wendell was fine. Tossing the toy into the water and having him lunge for it showed that he was incredibly brave (ahh, when faced with psycho dog-parent, first start with flattery), and his moment of confusion (i.e., drowning) was probably just due to his unfamiliarity with water. She then quizzed me about his "history" with water. I told her that he hated baths, avoided puddles, barked at the waves on the beach, and preferred Poland Spring to Evian.

For the next twenty minutes, as my own heart rate finally started to normalize, Marge and I watched Wendell run circles around the pool. It was obvious that Wendell had no plans ever to set foot in the water again if he could help it (thanks, Marge), though Marge seemed to think he really did want to try again but was now a bit gun-shy (gee, I wonder why). I had been taking pictures of Wendell next to the pool, but I found myself more than a little disappointed that I didn't have any pictures of Wendell actually *in* the water.

So here was the moment of truth in any parent's life. Did I now ask Marge to forcibly drag Wendell into the water just for the sake of a few pictures? (I'm pretty sure the definition of a Kodak moment does not include the word *terror*.) Or did I just call the whole thing a bust and leave with the consolation prize of being happy I didn't actually buy the eight-hundred-dollar digital video camera to record this non-moment in history?

It was then that Wendell put his front paws into the water on the first step, eyeing the fishy toy that was floating nearby, the very fishy toy that a half hour ago would have been his final undoing (if, say, his life were a Greek tragedy). Perhaps he was driven by blind rage and revenge. Perhaps he was truly brave, like Marge said, and now felt compelled to rescue the toy from the water. Or perhaps, and most likely, he just wanted to play with what was rightfully his.

This is when I asked Marge how she felt about bringing Wendell back into the water for one more try. She said she thought it was fine, and didn't even make a face when I scrambled to get ready by the side with my camera. By grabbing the fishy toy, she was then able to get a secure grip on Wendell, and with two large back steps she was now in the middle of the pool (the pool was like ten feet by ten feet, at best). Wendell struggled initially, but then seemed to relax in Marge's secure grip (either that, or he passed out from fear). Meanwhile my hands were going a mile a minute, snapping pictures like a pro (too bad we didn't have a wind machine, because rolling waves would have been a really nice effect). Through the lens I watched as Marge began to relax her grip on Wendell, and on cue Wendell began to pump his little legs. Soon he was totally on his own and was swimming like a champ toward the steps. Marge began to clap her hands and I cheered like the mom watching her child in the Olympics. It was truly a spectacular sight. And I have the pictures to prove it.

How to Buy a Birthday Cake for Your Dog

When you flip to the next month of your "365 Puppies a Year" wall calendar, stare first at the big picture of the "featured puppy of the month" and think to yourself that when your dog was a puppy he was definitely cuter than this scrawny little featured puppy, but not wanting to be caught thinking ill of another dog (bad canine karma), decide that this puppy is actually pretty cute, too. Move your eyes downward and notice the box of the day later in the month that has been meticulously colored in with a yellow Hi-Liter with the words WENDELL'S BIRTHDAY written in all caps followed by four exclamation points that have been punctuated with little hearts. Take a deep breath as you realize that your dog, your precious darling, will be turning two years old this month.

Feel some joy over this fact, as you love birthdays in general (though not your own as much lately as you are now in your thirties and having to use eye cream), but also feel some disbelief, as you can't believe that your furry baby is already celebrating his second birthday with you. Sigh over the fact that time seems to be going almost too fast and before you know it he'll be ten and all grown up and then you'll have to fear that each passing day is bringing him closer to his demise. Shake your head at this horrible thought and remind yourself to celebrate each day of your dog's life and not worry about such things, especially as worrying causes more wrinkles around the eyes.

Blink once or twice at the little yellow box and realize you now have less than two weeks to figure out what type of cake to get your dog and to decide whether you are going to have a party like you did for his first birthday. Smile at this thought—remember the Raspberry Snow Queen cake for twenty-four (you had leftovers for weeks, okay you're lying, you had leftovers for three days, but it was really good cake), the punch that was served in little Winnie-the-Pooh paper cups, the dalmatian napkins and paper plates, the little party hats that you forced on your friends and neighbors, the noisemakers, and the fact that your dog seemed to like wrapping paper and ribbon more than the gifts themselves (though didn't we all at that age?).

After giving yourself a mental pat on the back for putting together such a nice event last year, turn your thoughts toward the present-day cake situation and immediately have one of those eureka moments where you feel like you are the smartest person in the world at that very second when in all actuality you have not discovered the solution for world hunger but only have come to the rather obvious conclusion that since your dog happens to love ice cream, perhaps an ice-cream cake on his birthday would be nice. Call information to find the number of his favorite ice-cream parlor and then call.

The person who answers the phone sounds exactly how

you'd like someone who works in an ice-cream parlor to sound like and this makes you happy.

Say that you'd like to order a birthday cake. She says great and asks you how many people you plan on serving, as they have many different sizes. Tell her at this point in time you're not sure, but you're the type who'd rather have too much as opposed to too little, and make a lame joke about the fact that one can never have too much ice cream. Laugh at your own joke and she laughs, too, but know that her laugh is probably more from her sugar high from eating on the job than you being funny. Tell her you'd like to be able to serve at least twenty.

Next she tells you that you need to pick between vanilla and chocolate cake, and you immediately say that the cake can have no chocolate in it at all, as your . . . and this is the moment of truth where you have to decide if you should lie and say that this cake is for a person who is allergic to chocolate or just go ahead and tell the truth, that this particular cake happens to be for your dog's second birthday. By telling her it's for a dog you know that as soon as you get off the phone she'll have no choice but to go around and tell all her coworkers that some lady just ordered a cake for her dog (you realize there is not much excitement that goes on in ice-cream shops, so this might be big news). Somehow the fact that everyone will be yukking it up at the expense of your dog, whom they don't even know, makes you uncomfortable. After a moment's hesitation say that your *child* is allergic to chocolate.

Hear sympathetic clucking on the other end of the line, as of course any woman would find an allergy to chocolate to be quite tragic, and agree by saying, "Yes, sad, isn't it?" After a brief moment of silence where you are both thanking God that you yourselves do not have such an unfortunate allergy, she then tells you that you need to pick two different ice-cream flavors that will go in the cake. This is easy, as your dog has simple yet refined tastes when it comes to ice cream—vanilla and strawberry. She then tells you that in between the cake layer and the ice cream they usually put chocolate crunchies, but since your child is allergic then they can either forgo them altogether or replace them with something else. Ponder this for a moment and talk about caramel and butterscotch versus whipped cream or a strawberry glaze and then decide that maybe you should forgo it altogether as your d—uh, your child has a sensitive stomach and so it might be best to go as plain as possible.

The next thing on the form that she is filling out is whether or not you would like a message on the cake. Respond by saying yes, that you would like the cake to read "Happy Birthday" with your d—er, your child's name on it. Spell your dog's name twice just to be absolutely sure that there will be no icing typos on such an important day. You then ask what other decorations they do, as you would like the cake to be festive and pretty and you explain that your d—er, your child is male and so it would be best if the decorator didn't go overboard with the flowers, though one or two flowers would be okay as long as they aren't pink. At last, discuss price and pickup time and then say good-bye. Hang up the phone and feel pretty darn happy.

Now call your husband, best friend, or mom (if she's not the type to get annoyed that you would even get a birthday cake for your dog, which you think is totally fine especially as you don't have kids yet and you are in fact married and make your own money and are therefore allowed to do whatever you like with or without her approval) to share your good cake news, since you are not going to tell your dog, as you want it to be a surprise.

Your husband picks up the phone in that way that says he's very busy and you'd better talk fast, as he's about to tell you that he's too busy to talk to you so you tell him about the cake all in a rush without even pausing to take a breath and when you're done you hear your husband say something that totally throws you for a loop and in a voice that can only be described as a ten-year-old's, "What about the chocolate crunchies? The chocolate crunchies are the best part."

Make a face into the phone and say in your best mother of bratty ten-year-old voice, "Chocolate crunchies are chocolate. Dogs can't eat chocolate." A fact you've told him on numerous occasions, and just to get your point across you say, "Chocolate is poisonous to dogs, it could kill him." Hear a noise over the phone that sounds like an eight-year-old sucking in his bottom lip and since you can't stand the noise you say, "What? What? Just say it." Which then leads to him asking whether or not they could do half. Yes, that's what he actually asked, whether they could make *half* an ice-cream cake with chocolate crunchies. In disbelief, say, "HALF? HALF? LIKE HALF LIKE A PIZZA THAT HAS HALF PEPPER-ONI AND HALF CHEESE?" And then think that perhaps they *can* do it, because after all this is America, where everything is possible.

Say, "Fine, I will ask about the crunchies." And then say good-bye.

Call the ice-cream store again and feel relief when you get a different person. Wait until she looks up your order and then explain the request, which of course they don't seem to understand, because it is sort of weird to ask for half a cake to have crunchies while the other half does not. Listen as she keeps saying, "Half? You want half?" And then explain that one of the kids at the party is allergic to chocolate which is why you said no to the crunchies in the first place but then you found out that your husband really thinks that it's the crunchies that make an ice-cream cake, and he wanted to know if they could make half the cake with crunchies and half without. So then the woman who is now not as confused as she was before but is probably wondering how old my husband is to actually be so selfish as to endanger the life of a child at a birthday party proceeds to explain the nature of crunchies, which is that they are small, as well as crunchy, and that there could certainly be a chance that one or two errant crunchies might accidentally make their way over to the noncrunchy side and then get into the piece of cake that is given to the child with allergies and honestly would the death of a child really be worth it?

Decide that the particular scooper chick you happen to be speaking to is a bit too melodramatic and get slightly annoyed that she would think you were the type of person who would endanger the life of a child, so you say that the allergy is actually not that bad and that you personally plan on checking the piece of cake that goes to the d—er, you mean the child that has the allergy.

She then puts you on hold with the pretense of asking whether such a thing is possible, when she's really just telling everyone there about the crazy woman that she has on hold, who's endangering the life of a small child over a few lousy crunchies. After another minute she gets back on the phone and says that they will honor my request but that they want me to know that *they* don't think it's a good idea, *and* that they don't want to be held responsible if something were to happen. Assure the woman that everything will be fine and that you do not expect any problems and that you consider yourself to be the type of person who is very very careful, but if by chance something were to go horribly wrong at the party you would certainly never cast the blame on them. She says fine. Say fine back. And then you both hang up the phone.

Walk over to your calendar and in pen write "pick up cake twelve noon" in the little yellow box.

The 10 Breeds of Obsessed Dog Owners

4. The Owner Who Has Absolutely No Control over His Dog

It's just painfully obvious that the dog is the alpha in the relationship—the boss. Generally a bit sweaty and out of breath, this owner is always having to chase down their dog (that is, when not being *chased* by their dog as if they were prey). Instead of giving their dogs commands, these owners tend to ask permission for everything: "Do you want to go outside?" "Do you want to go home?" "Do you want to go through the McDonald's drive-through and get a double-cheeseburger combo meal?" You try to discourage your dog from hanging out with the dogs of such owners, mainly because these owners are a bad example for your dog, who can't help but get ideas. So whenever you part company with such a dog owner you'll want to pump up your own inner alpha as you bark "Don't even think about it" to your own dog.

Do You Often Worry About Your Dog's Reputation?

OPEN MOUTH, INSERT DOPPELGÄNGER

Cambridge is a pretty small dog town, and while I can't go so far as to say that I know *all* the dogs in my neighborhood, I can say I know most of them, especially the other wheaten terriers. From what I can gather there are at least another four or five wheaten terriers in the Harvard Square and Porter Square area—Lucy, who lives on the next street over and who happens to be quite petite for the breed and is half of Wendell's size; Guinness, who lives up Mass Ave on Avon Hill; the wheaten belonging to the Stonestreet store owner in Harvard Square (though she really lives in the burbs, commuting in from time to time to go to work with her owner); and then there's Barney, whom I haven't seen in quite a while—so long that I'm hoping that they moved away.

So I was pretty surprised one day to hear from a woman

who works near where I live that there's another wheaten that I haven't met yet who lives somewhere on our street.

Trying not to be impolite I asked again, "Are you sure this other wheaten lives on this street? It's just that I'm out and about a lot and I've never seen one."

The woman nodded vigorously, and explained how she's been having to work late a lot on a project and for the last three nights in a row she's seen a strange man with a wheaten who's bigger than Wendell on this street. Her answer to me not having ever seen him before was that perhaps the man takes the dog to work with him, so they're not around during the day. This was when she leaned in and of course, I leaned forward, eager to hear what else she knew. "Though the other option as to why you haven't seen him around is because maybe he didn't live here at all, and that maybe he was just in the neighborhood late at night visiting his mistress."

Now, at this revelation I was suddenly quite giddy with excitement, as my only regret about not having a normal day job these days is the lack of office gossip. And even though I'm a charter subscriber to Us Weekly, I know that gossiping about stars all the time is a bit tacky and I would much rather hear about the dirt on my neighbors.

"Really, what makes you think he's having an affair?" I shook my head at Wendell, who was sitting between us and moving his head back and forth like he was watching a tennis match. I could tell that my excited voice quality was making him excited, too.

She blushed at this, but only for a moment. "Well, obviously I can't be certain, but I know he's married because he wears a ring and it just seems like he's a little shifty."

A shifty man in the neighborhood with a wheaten, boy, this story was just getting better and better.

"Shifty how?"

"Well, he always seems to be in such a rush, hissing at the dog to hurry up and go to the bathroom, but meanwhile the poor dog obviously has issues of his own."

I loved this woman; she even had dirt on the dog.

"Tell me. Tell me."

"Well, let's just put it this way, his wheaten isn't as well trained as your darling Wendell. This man's wheaten doesn't seem to be trained at all—it's sort of wild, in fact. The dog is always growling and baring its teeth and it seems that they're always fighting. The guy has absolutely no control over the animal whatsoever."

The thought of a wheaten baring its teeth and being vicious really didn't sit well with me, as wheatens are known to be independent and strong spirited, but they are rarely aggressive. I put my hand over my mouth. "You don't think he abuses the poor thing?" I was almost feeling sick at the thought.

She gave me a wise eyebrow raise to show that she was not ruling out such a thing, because who knows what shifty characters are capable of. She tsked-tsked at the thought and told me that she wondered whether the dog might even know that his master was having an affair and didn't like it. Especially with dogs being so loyal and ethical.

I nodded at this, and as I was about to ask for a description of the guy she looked at her watch, realized that she was late for a meeting, and had to run off back to work. Disappointed that I couldn't hear more, but still pretty juiced up from everything I had just found out, I was now ready to run inside and do my duty by spreading the word. Looking down on the sidewalk I saw that Wendell was patiently lying at my feet, and when I squatted next to him he lifted his head and gazed at me adoringly.

I gave him a big under-the-chin rub and said, "Did you hear that, Wendell? You've got an evil twin lurking in the neighborhood with a big ol' scumbag for an owner. What do you think about that?" Wendell gave me a yawn to show that he was more interested in starting his afternoon nap than getting into a lengthy discussion of doppelgängers.

After Wendell was spread out on the futon couch behind my desk, I thought about whether or not I should call Cosmas and tell him the latest neighborhood murmurings, but I decided to tough it out instead and wait until he got home, as gossip is always so much better in person.

But later that afternoon I did get a chance to spread the word a bit while waiting in line at the small grocery market that was two blocks from my house. Lucky for me a woman who lived in the building across the street from me was standing behind me in line. I could tell she was wondering why I kept turning around and staring at her, so I finally introduced myself and told her that I lived at 12 Wendell, across the street from where she lived. She then feigned slight recognition and I could tell she was the type who didn't like small talk, but I proceeded anyway, assuming that the international currency of good gossip would soon win her over.

"So, I've got to ask whether you've seen a suspicious-looking guy with a wheaten terrier lurking around our street at night?"

The flicker of recognition couldn't be missed, but I could tell she was probably a stuffy New Englander who looked down upon gossip as bourgeois, so she was hesitating, trying to decide whether or not to go for it.

Desperate to get the ball rolling, I decided to throw out the nugget that no red-blooded woman who was alive in the era of Alexis Morrell Carrington Colby Dexter Rowan (Joan Collins's character on *Dynasty*) could forgo: "I mean, I'm only asking because I've heard that he's wrapped up in some illicit affair"—I looked around, pretending to make sure that no one was listening, just to ratchet up the tension, and then I leaned back in—"and I hear he's *this* close to getting busted by his wife." Hmmm, now that was sort of interesting, who knew I could lie so well? I guess this was exactly how rumors got out of control. This was when I turned forward to show that if she didn't want to partake in the most interesting news to hit this street since the yellow house two doors down from her had a kitchen fire, then so be it.

"So are *we* talking about the guy with the rabid dog?" Her voice was low, not wanting to get caught, but she did use the universal gossip pronoun of *we*, which showed she knew how the game was played.

I brought my mouth in a round O and let my eyes widen appropriately, rewarding her naughty ways with lots of positive affirmation. "The dog is rabid?"

At this she sniffed, and did a little ahem into her hand and said, "Well, I don't know if it's a wheaty terrier or whatever you called it, but there is some man who always walks this overgrown furball dog late at night; and this dog, well, he's basically crazy. Jumping about like an animal straight from the jungle, like it's never been leashed before. Obviously, I'm assuming the poor beast isn't really rabid, but whatever he's got, it's not good."

Now it was my turn in line and I smiled at the cashier, who smiled at me, and was obviously waiting for us to continue with the story.

I then went on to explain that I felt rather foolish that I had never encountered the man with the Tarzan dog, especially as I had my own dog, and that this was all apparently happening right under my own nose—well, at least under my own window. In the next breath I went on to defend myself by saying that I never walked my dog late at night, as that was my husband's responsibility, but that I had every intention of getting to the bottom of the affair (I got extra gossip points for this comment—we like puns).

So then the three of us (the cashier was now involved) proceeded to get all up in arms over the whole idea that a man would not only cheat on his wife, but would also use the feeble "taking the dog out for a walk" as his excuse. (The cashier got in a great zing, saying that it was obvious he was taking more than just his dog out for a walk, and, girlfriend, we knew what she meant!) The cashier then speculated that perhaps he just got the dog from a shelter for the sole purpose of using it to hide his evil ways. My neighbor sympathized with the poor wife, speculating that perhaps she knew her husband was having an affair, but was afraid to say something out of fear that her husband might sic the dog on her. And I wondered who on earth the guy could be having an affair with, as I felt I had a pretty good handle on most of my neighbors. All in all, it was the most fun I've had grocery shopping in a while.

Walking home with my neighbor, we changed the subject just in case Hester Prynne happened to be out and about, and we finished up our discussion with the standard neighborly fare—lack of street parking and the fact that it made no sense that people honked their horns at the garbage truck when it was obvious that there was no way they could pass it anyway. We parted in front of her house with promises that we'd both be keeping our eyes and ears open, and then I waved and walked home.

That night over dinner I mentioned to Cosmas that maybe he and I should switch walking Wendell for a week or so, and that I'd take the last walk if he would do the first walk in the morning (it goes without saying that I always do the two walks in the afternoon since I am home during the day). Cosmas asked why I wanted to switch, but I just gave my best casual shrug and said I needed a little change, that was all. After much thought on my part I decided that involving

Cosmas in the whole thing was probably not the wisest move, as for all I knew Cosmas would feel some sort of code among men and decide to tell the adulterer that the neighborhood gossips were on to him and that he'd better watch his back. I also was now a bit nervous over Wendell's safety because God forbid, if the man's crazy dog attacked Wendell, I figured I'd be better equipped to handle the situation than Cosmas, especially considering that Wendell never really heeded Cosmas's commands.

Cosmas shrugged at my shrug and said it was fine by him.

For the next five nights I took Wendell out at different times from 11:30 P.M. until 1:30 in the morning, but I never once saw anything suspicious at all. I was disappointed, to say the least, but with each passing day I began to wonder whether perhaps the man had come to his senses and ended his affair, or perhaps the dog was indeed rabid and possibly had bitten the man, who was now having to undergo the very painful process of getting shots in the stomach, and finally I realized that perhaps there was no affair, shifty man, or crazy dog at all.

On the following Saturday during Wendell's midafternoon walk I was passing by the grocery store and saw that my neighbor was in the store, and so I quickly decided to tie Wendell outside and go in and inquire whether she had had any better luck spotting the mystery man.

When I approached her in the produce section I could tell that she wasn't exactly happy to see me, since she had a sort of stricken look on her face as I came bounding through the front door and gave her a big wave. I assumed that she was the type who didn't want others to know of her penchant for gossip (to each her own, I guess) and of course I didn't want to out her among the produce, so I gave her a sly wink and quickly picked up an avocado to use as a decoy. And everyone knows a good guacamole needs a little bit of onion, so soon I was standing right next to her at the onion bin, where I whispered a hello.

She responded with a cursory nod, and took two steps to the left and was now perusing the tomatoes. I, now holding an onion as well, scooted two steps over toward the tomatoes, too, thinking she was playing hardball.

"So, have you seen our guy? I've been cruising all week and I'm running on fumes." I smiled, always loving any opportunity to talk like a spy. (Move on over, Nikita, La Femme Jenn is here.)

Again she responded by taking two steps away from me, and this time it was obvious that she wasn't playing along. Instead of pushing the matter, I decided to bail, as no one likes a pushy gossip, and of course the first rule of gossip is that it should be fun. So even though I was a little hurt, I put on a brave face and turned toward the registers, bidding her a quiet good-bye.

"I saw him again." Her voice was low, but luckily my hearing has always been sharp. I resisted the urge to whip around, as it was now clear that her little two-step maneuver moments ago was just her way of building the tension so she could be queen of the gossip mound, especially since I walked in mouthing off how I had nothing, so I turned slowly, trying to stay very casual.

"Really?" I didn't push it further than that, as it wasn't like I was going to beg (well, I was, but it wasn't as if she had to know that).

She stood her ground. Dammit, she was good.

I jingled my keys a bit, just to break up the tension and to give her a little audible signal indicating I was more than prepared to walk away—which meant that she would be left with nothing but the grapefruit she was holding. Everybody knows that gossip is a two-way street.

She scowled a bit but continued, "I didn't see him with the dog. And I saw him in the morning."

Well, it was obvious that she was going with the no-frills approach, but I had to admit that seeing him in the morning was pretty big news. *Caught in the walk of shame? Had he left his wife and moved in with his floozy mistress? Maybe there was no affair and he just happened to live in the area.* Since she had earned it, I had to give it to her; and since I had to give it to her, I gave it to her good.

"NO WAY! YOU SAW HIM IN THE MORNING?! DO YOU KNOW WHAT THAT MEANS? WOW. YOU'RE KIDDING. WHEN? SO NO DOG, HUH? INTERESTING, VERY VERY INTERESTING."

She accepted my congratulatory chatter with steely smugness, and then proceeded to tell me all she knew. She, too, had not seen him at night since we had last spoken, which made me happy, as I would have been horrified to have missed him on my watch. She said that she knows she saw him on Wednesday because it was trash day and she was downstairs in the street making sure that the trash men didn't throw her cans all around and scuff them up. That's when she saw him, but it was only for a second.

Still a bit bitchy from the earlier snub, I had to ask, "How did you know it was him if he didn't have the dog?" I felt this was a fair question, especially since previously she had seen him only at night from her second-floor window.

Her reply was simple: "I knew it was the same shifty man because of the beard and glasses." She then gave the grapefruit she was holding a little *nyah-nyah* squeeze for emphasis.

At this news, I was suddenly wary, because the way I saw it, the fact that she was only just now revealing that she had even had such precise physical attributes of the man in question was a bit odd. Why hadn't she mentioned the glasses and a beard last week? Seriously, glasses and a beard was big stuff, well, not as big as say a mustache and a cowboy hat, but close enough. Though, granted, this was Cambridge, home of Harvard and MIT—capital of disheveled professors with worn elbow patches, chalky pants, and beards and glasses. I mean, after all, even my own husband was sporting a beard these days.

Annoyed that I hadn't yet cheered over her news, she let the final bomb drop; she added, "And, if you must know, I saw him coming out of *your* building."

With this news, the whole terrifying truth came to light, and I was about to totally lose it, when I was saved by the bark. I whipped around at the sound, quickly apologized for my hasty retreat, and ran to the checkout aisle, then paid for my stuff and left before I could hear any more.

Outside I quickly untied Wendell and headed home, my mind racing. Yes, I've been known to suspend disbelief in the name of good gossip, and maybe, just maybe I could believe that there was a second wheaten terrier owned by some mystery man who lived or was sleeping with someone on my street, who also happened to have glasses and a beard, but there was no way—like NONE—that such a thing could be going on in my own building without me knowing. Which meant only one thing. That the mystery man was my husband (and for those of you too slow to keep up, obviously, he's *not* having an affair), and even worse, the mystery dog was my own Wendell. (How nice to learn from a random stranger that your own dog has a split personality.)

When I got home I found Cosmas sitting on the couch, and not wanting to drag the whole thing out any longer, I walked right over, sat down on the couch next to him, took the remote out of his hand, and turned off the television. He was about to object until he saw that I had my snake-eyes face on.

"What? I just got home." Implying that there was no way he could already have gotten in trouble.

Not knowing the best way to start, I just came right out and said it.

"I think you should know that some of the people in the neighborhood seem to think that you are having an affair."

Cosmas's eyes went wild, and I pushed forward, not giving him a chance to interrupt. "Of course I know it isn't true, and I guess it's just a big case of mistaken identity. Let's just chalk it up to the doppelgänger effect and not worry about it, okay? But I thought you might want to know this just in case you get some funny or weird looks." I paused, took a deep breath, and quickly changed the subject. "Are you hungry? I was thinking about making some guacamole."

In hindsight I realized I should have left the TV on to tell him this, as the distraction would have probably slowed down his reaction time, but it was too late and he was able to grab my arm right as I was about to flee. Drats.

"What are you talking about? I have a doppelgänger?"

I sighed, now annoyed that my own doppelgänger had such a big mouth.

"It's really complicated, and not all that interesting. . . . Y'know, did I mention that I found those really good corn chips that you like? I might even have sour cream, too." Strike two on the subject change, which was just as well, since I was lying about the sour cream.

"Okay, from what I can gather, it seems that some people in the neighborhood reported seeing some shifty guy late at night with a wild dog that happened to look a lot like Wendell." I got up off the couch and headed toward the kitchen to start making the guacamole and Cosmas followed. "But given the fact that Wendell isn't wild, it was just assumed that he had an evil doppelgänger."

I started peeling the avocado and motioned to Cosmas to

hand me the lemon juice, which he handed to me, but when I grabbed it he didn't let go. I looked up and he met my eyes full on. "So you mean to tell me that our neighbors think I look weird?"

I rolled my eyes—such a man to turn the whole conversation back to him. I ignored his question and just continued mashing up the avocado in a bowl. Wendell had now appeared in the kitchen and was lying by my feet looking up toward the counter, hoping that I would drop the masher, the bowl, or both (Wendell loved avocado). Cosmas picked a piece out of the bowl and gave it to Wendell and then nudged me to continue.

So I did. "And while I was at the store just now I just found out that the doppelgänger dog's owner had glasses and a beard, which then led me to realize that maybe it wasn't actually a doppelgänger at all, but in fact, was our own wild dog. . . ." I spooned up some guac and gave it to Cosmas to taste. He nodded in a way that meant it needed to be spicier, so I reached for the Tabasco and continued, "Which now leads me back to you, as I'd love to hear why people describe Wendell as rabid when he's with you." Finally, I could tell by Cosmas's expression that I had gotten a hit, which was now soaring toward the outfield. The way I saw it was that Cosmas could catch the ball and call me out and pursue the avenue of why it was that people would make the leap from having a wild dog to having an affair, or he could call it a game and let me off the hook (because, duh, it's so obvious that I was somehow to blame for the whole thing), thereby getting himself off the hook for having to explain why it was that he had no control over our dog at night.

Cosmas called sudden death, which obviously didn't really work with my baseball analogy, but Cosmas didn't watch sports anyway. Sudden death was a game we invented for the times that we are on opposing sides on an issue that could easily either turn into a big fight (Cosmas hated to fight with me, as I was much more skilled with words and talked fast) or would take a long time to resolve (Cosmas hated long, drawn-out discussions, too), and it involved us having to finish discussing whatever the topic in question was in three short rounds and then we had to drop the subject immediately.

"Fine, you go first." In sudden death, it was better to go second.

"The whole affair thing is basically your fault, right?"

I nodded. "Sixty-five percent me, thirty-five percent other, but let the record show that it did not originate with me." It was my turn to ask a question, and the rules said that it didn't have to be related to the current strand of questioning. "Is Wendell out of control with you at night because you never discipline him and now he thinks you are weak and takes advantage?"

He nodded. "Yes. One hundred percent." We liked adding in numbers, it sounded more spy-like. "Is there anything else about my evil double that I should know? Have I fathered a child?"

"No. One hundred percent. Well, not that I know of.

Eighty percent. It'll all blow over, trust me. So, how would you feel if I made you and Wendell go to obedience school for a refresher course?"

"I would be annoyed. Ninety percent. Do I have any choice in this matter?"

"Not really. Eighty-five percent. The other two options are to move, or shave your beard and get contacts."

Cosmas shaved his beard but refused to get contacts (he thought eyeballs were gross), I changed grocery stores, and it was agreed that I would continue to walk Wendell in the evenings; well, at least until obedience school started.

How to Tell If You're Obsessed with Your Dog

Ignore all the obvious signs of dog obsession, like the fact you really feel your dog has been slightly depressed as of late and have been wondering whether he is going through some sort of existential crisis and even had a two-hour phone conversation with your friend Victoria (proud mamma of Atticus and Nina) to discuss this issue as well as all other minutiae having to do with our darling dogs. *Really? Atticus prefers the beef-flavored toothpaste? Hmmm, maybe I'll try that for Wendell. I just went safe and got the peanut-butter one but I do think that brushing with peanut butter seems so bizarre, it's like that little-kid toothpaste that comes in bubblegum flavor. Don't you find that just wrong?* Also dismiss the fact that when you were driving your husband to work this morning and the Peter Cetera song "You're the Inspiration" came on the radio, you had the distinct feeling that you were both singing the song with particular gusto, not to each other, but to your dog, who was standing in between you—half in the backseat and half in the front seat (never mind that you bought a car specifically to accommodate the fact that he likes to stand on the armrest between the two of you in the classic *Titanic* pose).

In fact, don't even care that you know all of your friends are getting a little tired of your precious oh-by-the-way-did-I-tell-you-what-darling-thing-Wendell-did-today stories (jealousy is such an ugly emotion, don't you think?). Never give a thought to the fact that your social calendar now revolves around your latest fear that if your dog is alone for more than five hours by himself he might just succeed in watching enough movies on cable to finally figure out how to open the fridge or operate a dead bolt.

Say *pshaw* over the raised eyebrows that you get when you ask the sales clerks in furniture stores who they would recommend for designing a special custom chair for your dog that is the perfect width so that he can stretch out fully and not feel cramped, ever (adding that the armrest needs to be the exact length of his neck so that if he chooses to perch it on the armrest in a lackadaisical movie-star I'm-so-bored-but-aren't-I-fabulous-to-look-at way he is in a correct ergonomic position).

Continue this denial of certifiable dog obsession quite happily until the afternoon when you are coming back from a most disappointing playtime at the park, where you waited in vain for almost an hour with hopes that another dog would show up for some rough-and-tumble playtime (c'mon, can't these other owners think of someone other than themselves for a change?), and where you tried to make up for his disappointment by running all over the park yourself, chasing after a ball like it was your mission in life (your dog is never interested in toys unless someone else is, too). Admit to yourself that this is probably your own way of assuaging your guilt, as you know that your dog will be all by his lonesome for the evening as you have no choice but to see your friend for dinner since you've already canceled on her twice before because of your dog's emotional state.

As you walk into your building you stop to check the mail and right as you're cursing the fact that all you seem to get are bills and junk mail, you get one of those weird inklings—the one that if your life were a movie and you were the main character you'd see a flashback of the moment where your fate could have changed if only you had done one little thing differently when you had the chance. Your one-little-thing moment is that when you were walking down the steps an hour previous you did manage to see out of the corner of your eye a little white pill lying on the right side of the first step and you remember thinking that you should probably pick it up because God knows what it is, where it's been, and what if your darling pooch found it, ingested it, and promptly died. But of course you didn't pick it up then because you were feeling all anxious and in a rush to get to the park just in case there happened to be a whole pack of dogs playing right that very moment and you were going to miss them all if you didn't hurry.

At this time you hear a *sniff, sniff, crunch* sound echo through the foyer, reminiscent of *snap-crackle-pop* trapped in a Jamaican steel drum. Freeze for a moment and fall into a pit of denial for one glorious moment and then realize that even though free falls are sort of fun you realize that eventually you're going to hit the bottom and it's going to hurt like hell.

Start to scream as you look over your shoulder and see that the little white pill is gone and that your dog definitely has it in his mouth. Rack your brain and think of all the different things a little white pill could be—aspirin, Percocet, ecstasy, Valium (though you do think they are normally yellow or light blue so it's probably not that), or maybe even cyanide. Fast forward to page 34 of your ASPCA dog-health manual where it says that contrary to popular belief, you shouldn't give dogs aspirin, even if you think they have a headache. Rewind back to an hour earlier when you had first seen the pill and try to remember whether there was some sort of pattern on it, a symbol perhaps, and decide that yes, perhaps there was indeed a symbol on it (though c'mon, it's doubtful your vision is that good). Decide that it is ecstasy, as you know for a fact that you have a lot of twenty-year-olds in your building and you think you heard them going out late last night and since they were probably already on drugs at the time decide that they probably dropped one of their stash on the way out the door to go to a dance club.

Get really really annoyed at yourself—incensed even— *WHY DIDN'T I PICK UP THE DAMN THING WHEN I SAW IT EARLIER? I'M SO STUPID! I'M SO LAZY. HOW COULD I BE SO STUPID?!! HOW COULD I BE SO LAZY?!!*

Know that you don't have much time, so jump the four feet across the vestibule toward your dog and lunge for him. As your dog is no dummy and knows what you're going for he clamps down his jaw in a you-better-be-bionic-lady-because-there's-no-chance-of-you-prying-open-my-mouth-to-get-the-goods way. Scream "Bring it on" as you now have him sandwiched in between your legs and are prying open his mouth like Popeye with a can of spinach. Shove your whole hand into his mouth and try to wipe off his tongue and watch as a big piece of the pill goes flying to the floor. Continue to rub his tongue, trying to wipe off the residue, and wonder whether this action will backfire as you are actually grinding it into his tongue and making it dissolve faster.

Assume that there is already enough of the poison in him and think about whether you should lug his furry butt outside and force-feed him some grass to make him throw up and then remember that there is some sort of stuff that I can never pronounce that you can buy at a drugstore that you can give a person to make him throw up just in case of such an occasion. Think *WHY DON'T I HAVE ANY OF THAT POISON-ANTIDOTE THROW-UP STUFF AT HOME? WHY AM I NOT BETTER PREPARED? HOW CAN I BE SO STUPID?*

Watch as your dog has now managed to wriggle his way out from behind you as you are wiping your hands on your jeans. See that the bigger half of whatever it was is now lying on the ground two feet away on your right. Notice that your dog has also spotted it and is preparing to dive after it himself, as he figures that if you obviously don't want him to have it then it must be the best thing ever. Throw yourself down onto the floor and hope that your five-foot-four-inch body has managed to cover the tiny four-millimeter pill. Know you were successful on your mission, as your dog is now literally digging at your side with both paws as if you are a bed of dirt. Yell at the top of your lungs, "NO EAT! NO EAT! NO EAT!"

Gyrate your body into the ground in a most embarrassing way and get a good EPOC (estimated point of contact) with the poison in question. Roll suddenly to the left toward your dog, throwing him off balance, and grab for it with your left hand in one sudden movement as if you were in a slick John Woo movie. Next, lick the palm of your right hand and slap the ground in an attempt to pick up any of the crumbs. Do it again. As you slap your hand the second time think about the fact that you have basically just licked the floor of the vestibule of your apartment building where forty-odd people and four other dogs have walked. Think about the fact that your hand was already pretty dirty from picking up the slimy ball in the park and the fact that thirty seconds ago your entire hand was in your dog's mouth. Let the enormity of it all wash over you. *I CAN'T BELIEVE I JUST LICKED MY HAND! I CAN'T BELIEVE I JUST BASICALLY LICKED THIS DIRTY FLOOR. OHMYGOD THIS IS LIKE FEAR FACTOR WITHOUT THE CHANCE OF WINNING MONEY! WHEN WAS MY LAST TETANUS SHOT?*

While you are thinking that your last tetanus shot was probably well over ten years prior, your brain suddenly registers something—some flavor. Work your tongue around your mouth to confirm the flavor.

Mint.

Realize what you are tasting besides dirt and shoe scum is indeed mint, perhaps even a curiously strong one, maybe an Altoid? Open your fist and stare at the tiny jagged shard of mint, put your nose to it and smell just to make sure. Nod to yourself, yes, it's definitely a mint. Think back to your dog-health manual and try to recall whether mint is bad for dogs. Think about the fact that human toothpaste is not good for dogs, but that is due to the fluoride and not the minty taste. Pick yourself off the ground and try not to look at the fact that you are now a walking load of dirty laundry. Look at your dog, who is now sitting before you like an angel with hopes that he can have the rest of the mint that is in your hand. *Hmmmm, maybe I should see if there is mint-flavored toothpaste for dogs, as he obviously likes it. Note to yourself to discuss with Victoria.*

Sigh and give your dog the mint and watch as he happily crunches away and then swallows it. Smile that he seems happy and watch him wag his tail. Say, good dog. Walk up the stairs toward your apartment and replay what just happened in your head once more. Laugh and decide that perhaps you might be just a little obsessed when it comes to your dog. 🐾

BYE-BYE BLACKBIRD

Cosmas has always been in charge of the last walk of the evening, and more often than not he has grumbled. I have tried over the months to give it a positive spin by explaining that a little late-night carousing was male bonding at its finest, but Cosmas doesn't always buy what I'm selling—and on this particular evening he was cranky enough to even snap back, "He's a dog, okay?"

I didn't respond out loud, but in my head I was playing the world's smallest violin solo of "My Heart Bleeds for You"—I mean, we were talking about one freakin' walk a day (if you can *even* call four minutes of pacing by the side of our apartment building a walk), whereas I walk Wendell (with total joy and glad tidings) at least three times a day, plus I feed him, plus I comb him, plus I give him at least two belly-rubs a day, plus I give him treats . . . but who's counting? Instead I held steadfast and just watched Cosmas walk out the door in a huff, with Wendell trotting after him—Wendell did shoot me a quick backward glance as if to say, "What's up Daddy's butt?" and I just winked, shrugged, and gave him a little wave so as not to worry his furry little head about it.

So when Cosmas and Wendell didn't come back inside within their normal five minutes, I just assumed that Cosmas was doing penance for his ridiculous "He's a dog, okay" comment and was perhaps actually walking Wendell around the entire block, or at least down our street and back.

When they had been gone for what seemed like almost

twenty minutes (the walk up and down the street is seven minutes, the shortcut walk around the block is eleven, and the entire block is eighteen), I stood up to go look out the window. Our apartment faces the street, and being on the third floor in combination with the fact that I'm not afraid of heights allowed me the usefulness of leaning out the window and being able to see down most of the street. Right when I lifted the window screen and was about to lean out of the window was when I heard the front door of the building slam.

Next, I heard running on the stairs, which made my breath catch, but then I exhaled noisily, knowing that it would take an elephant stampede to ever get Cosmas to run up the stairs. A second later our door flew open, Cosmas came barreling in with Wendell tucked under his arm as if he were a football, and I watched as he quietly closed the door behind him and was now staring out of the peephole.

I was soon by his side, and I pushed him gently aside so that I could see if there really was an elephant standing in our hallway. There wasn't.

Wendell was now struggling to get free, probably embarrassed that he was even caught in such a puppyish position by me, and I tapped Cosmas on the shoulder and without making a sound motioned that he should put Wendell on the floor. I squatted to take his collar off and was surprised to see Wendell exercising defiance by not sitting like he normally does. I narrowed my eyes at him, the same look I shoot Cosmas when I catch him about to chug straight from the orange-juice container . . . and Wendell sat. Now that's more like it.

Cosmas had finally caught his breath and asked whether I thought anyone heard him come in. So I was wondering whether he meant if anyone in, say, the People's Republic of China heard him—probably not, since it was like 5:00 A.M. there, and surely even Communists don't have to get up that early, but everyone in our twenty-four-unit apartment building had certainly heard him. But I informed him that there was no way anyone would have thought it was him (Cosmas's work schedule is such that most people don't even know I have a husband), that is, unless he was talking to Wendell on his way up.

Cosmas shook his head no, and I noticed that it looked like his forehead was sweating.

"What happened out there?" For some reason my voice was very calm, even though I was getting increasingly nervous over Cosmas's twitchiness. I was the drama queen of the family, and Cosmas was the laid-back one (laid back, disinterested, call it whatever you like), so it was more than a bit disconcerting to have Cosmas acting in this fashion, and I don't know if I had ever really heard Cosmas whisper before.

"So I went out to walk Wendell . . ."—I tried to keep my eyes from rolling, duh, this I knew, but I said nothing—"and he did his business pretty quick, and when we were on our way back in, he didn't want to go, and instead started pulling me toward the Harvard Law lot [the little patch of grass that is in front of the dorm building to the left of our building].

So I figured maybe he had to go again. . . . So then all of sudden he starts doing that crouchy thing, you know, when he looks like a lion on the hunt."

I smiled at this, as I loved when Wendell did his crouchy stalking thing; you should see him, how he crouches really low, his little back flat, taking three or four crouchy steps and then freezing, and then taking three or four more . . . it's truly darling.

At this we both paused and looked around for Wendell, who happened to be sitting a few feet away by his water bowl, patiently waiting for us to notice that it was almost empty. (Wendell doesn't like the dregs.) I moved to fill his bowl and told Cosmas to go on.

"So then I see that there is a large black bird just standing at the far side of the grass."

My eyebrows lifted up, much in the way of a bird lifting off the ground in flight. "Large black bird? What, like a crow?" As far as I knew there were no crows in Cambridge. But then again I wasn't sure whether I had ever even seen a crow in my life, I mean, is every bird that is black a crow? There is a bird that is called a blackbird, right? As in "Bye Bye Blackbird"? All I knew about crows was that they liked corn, right? I mean, wasn't that where the whole scarecrow thing came from? I also had vague recollections of a cartoon crow that wore a hat and possibly even smoked a pipe. . . . When I looked up at Cosmas he was shaking his head.

"Bigger," he whispered, and then proceeded to hold out his arms to show the width of about five feet.

I couldn't help but snort a bit unattractively here. "Cosmas, that's like one mongo bird you saw. Is that the wingspan or the size of the actual bird? The only black bird that I know that is bigger than a crow is a raven, and I doubt those are the size of Christina Ricci, who's short, and besides, I don't think there are ravens in Cambridge, but then again it is almost Halloween. Maybe it's like a raven convention, or perhaps they were on their way to Salem but took a wrong turn somewhere." I snorted again at my own wit.

"Can I finish my story? I don't think you realize the gravity of the situation."

Right as I was about to protest the fact that he didn't think my raven Halloween joke was amusing and that half the battle with good storytelling came down to the descriptions, "You've got to make me feel like I was right there. Sure it was easy to imagine Wendell in his darling stalking crouchy-lion mode, but to imagine him stalking a giant black bird of some unknown origin was a little harder . . ."

"He killed it."

"What?" I shrieked, probably sounding like a crow myself.

"Dead. Wendell killed the bird." Cosmas was whispering again.

Now my eyes were big and suddenly I felt myself starting to sweat as well. I stammered, "What? I mean, how did he . . . ? I mean, are you sure? What happened?"

"Like I've been trying to tell you, he started doing the stalking thing, and since it was so late I let his leash go. . . ." At this I raised my eyebrows, and normally I'd start screaming about the fact that he let his leash go right near the street and Wendell could have gotten run over, but I let it go and let him continue. "So there he is stalking, stalking, stalking"— Cosmas is one of those people who you are surprised to find out has quite an extensive vocabulary— "and I kept waiting for the bird to notice him and fly away but it just sort of stood there, and all of a sudden Wendell pounced on it."

You know when you are young and the grossest thing you can ever imagine is your parents having sex, the involuntary cringe, how you shut your eyes and can't help but groan? This was worse. My hand was now over my mouth and I was absolutely horrified. Never in a million years could I imagine our darling Wendell killing a bird.

Hell, I still remember the shock I felt when he "killed" his first squeaky toy. Wendell was probably only eight months old and I was in New York City for the weekend and staying at my friend Phil's apartment. It was a Friday night and I had plans to go out with my best friend, Laura, and Phil had agreed to look after Wendell for the evening since he was having friends over for a poker game anyway. Right before I left I gave Wendell a new toy that I had found at the dog spa on Eighteenth Street; it was a stuffed bug with six dangling legs, bulging eyes, and the requisite squeaker. Five hours later when I got back to the apartment all was quiet. Wendell was asleep on the couch next to Phil, who was watching some random movie on his mammoth TV. I asked first how his game went (good—he won) and then I asked how Wendell was (good). Relieved, I sat down to see what he was watching, which is when I made the fatal error of complimenting Phil on the sound of the TV. So for the next ten minutes I was ordered to sit in every possible seat in the apartment—the other couch, the ottoman, the dining-room table, leaning over the kitchen counter, to marvel at how amazing the surround sound really was—"Oooh, so clear. Wow, it sounds like I'm right in the action [the movie was *Black Hawk Down*]. Really cool, I mean, if you get one size up in TV screen size you probably wouldn't even feel the need to go to the movies ever." (The update is that Phil has recently bought an LCD projector so he can project onto the wall of his loft apartment—honestly, and guys make fun of us about liking shoes?)

Anyway, it was from the vantage point of the kitchen that I first saw it. I remember squinting, wondering if my eyes were playing tricks on me, as I heard that's what sometimes happens during the stress of battle (the movie was really that loud). After blinking a few times I realized that yes, right in the shadows of the giant palm tree planter there was what appeared to be a little stuffed bug leg, just the leg. So my jaw dropped and I walked over horrified, and soon I was clutching a little dismembered bug leg in my hand and confronting Phil.

"What is this?" I waved the little leg with a little foot around.

"A leg." Phil waved me aside, as I was now blocking the picture.

"Why am I holding a leg?"

Phil shrugged. "War is hell?"

"This is so not funny, Phil, you need to tell me what went on here tonight. . . ." I trailed off as I just saw another leg by the far wall, and next to it was an eyeball. By this time I was pretty hysterical, as I had never once seen Wendell act so violently with a toy, and I was just about to try to figure out whether they had war movies on all night because I was going to maybe start to believe those alarmist people who say that violent movies do cause kids (and maybe dogs) to be more violent, when Phil finally admitted (easiest way to get me to shut up) that "some of the guys" had taught Wendell tug-of-war (the one game all the books say you should never play with your dog, great).

Later, after I had recovered from the shock of it all, I had bought another bug toy for Wendell and watched as Wendell meticulously ripped it apart—how he pulled off its eyes and nose first, callously almost spitting them aside, how he ripped off a few legs, and then finally as he pulled out all the stuffing until the thing was just a limp outer casing of a bug.

I was pulled out of my memory as Cosmas continued with his story. "So he pounced on it and then started batting it around. . . ." This was where I began to shake my head for him to stop talking. Suddenly I felt nauseous. A moment of silence passed.

Finally I whispered, my voice cracked, "Are you sure he killed it?"

Cosmas nodded. "Well, it was just lying there after I managed to grab the leash and pull Wendell away."

"Did he rip off a wing or a leg?"

Cosmas cringed. "No! That's disgusting, how could you say such a thing?"

I shrugged. "Well, you've seen him with his toys, anything that is not attached well is normally lying on the floor." I shivered with a bad case of the heebie-jeebies. Then another thought occurred to me. "Was there blood?" Without waiting for his reply I wildly looked around for Wendell, my precious baby, who was now a killer. Wendell had gone ahead and jumped into bed, and when I walked into the room and turned on the light, he lifted his head and gave me his normal friendly look. I walked over to him and rubbed under his chin, fearful that I'd find blood, feathers, and dead-bird germs, but there was nothing there (yes, I know you can't see germs, but let's not go there, okay?).

Cosmas had followed me to the bedroom but was standing in the doorway.

"It was awful. I mean, I just can't believe he'd kill a bird."

I closed my eyes again at the thought, though I must admit the idea of Wendell, who isn't even two feet tall, attacking a massive black bird with the wingspan of Yao Ming . . . I couldn't really see it. I mean, sure, Wendell is quite feisty, and I pity the yippy dog that meets up with him in a dark alley, but I'm not sure whether I felt he could take on a bird the size of Mothra. Suddenly I pictured Wendell on the back of a gigantic black bird the size of a dragon, flying off in the dark of night.

I turned around. "How do you know he really killed it? Maybe it was just pretending to be dead, like a possum."

"Like a what?" Cosmas was now clipping his nails at the kitchen table (gross nervous tic), and I walked over and got a paper towel and handed it to him. He looked at it for a moment and seemed confused, but then figured out that I wanted him to put his yicky clippings on the paper towel. Duh.

"A possum. You know, playing possum. It means playing dead, that's what they do. It's a defensive move that it does when under attack."

Finally Cosmas spoke. "I don't think it's nice to say that Wendell was attacking this big black bird, I think he was just playing with it."

"WHATEVER. I DON'T CARE WHETHER OR NOT HE WAS PLAYING WITH IT OR WHETHER HE'S A HIT MAN FOR THE *WILD KINGDOM* MOB. WHAT I WANT TO KNOW IS WHETHER OR NOT YOU INSPECTED THE BIRD TO SEE WHETHER IT WAS TRULY DEAD!"

Cosmas threw up his hands at this. "I am a doctor, you know, so I think I know when something is dead."

"Yes, I know you are a *human* doctor, but last I checked you weren't a vet. How did you know?"

Cosmas sounded suddenly tired. "Well, if you're asking whether I went over to feel its pulse, no, I didn't. But if you want to go out and hold a mirror to its, er, beak, then be my guest."

I put my hands on my hips and retorted, "I mean, I'd hardly think that one pounce and a couple of slaps would really kill this mighty winged creature."

Cosmas sighed. "I don't think the words 'mighty winged creature' ever came out of my mouth, okay? Your whole exaggeration thing in times of distress is normally cute, but tonight it's annoying. Just trust me that the big bird is dead, okay?"

"Did you nudge it with your foot afterward?" I had to ask, as I'm the type that needs to know all the facts.

"Ugh, no way." Cosmas was the most squeamish doctor I had ever encountered; you should see him try to kill a bug.

It was then that Wendell did a little snore thing, followed by combination roll over and stretch. Nice to know that he wasn't sweating any of this.

"Look at him, what a love bug." Cosmas leaned over the bed and gave Wendell a little rub.

"Yeah, love bug by day, sociopathic psychokiller by night." I looked up and immediately could see that Cosmas did not find this statement funny, but I didn't have time to apologize, as I was now on to bigger matters.

If Wendell really did kill some giant bird, then that meant its body was still lying in the yard, the same yard that all our neighbors walk by. I told Cosmas that we had to go out and dispose of the body. Explaining that because our building was so gossipy, everyone unable to mind their own business, always discussing every little detail of everyone's lives—who's new in the building, who had some girl sleep over, and who subscribed to which magazines (of course this was mainly me who did these things, but whatever)—I told him that the last thing we needed to deal with was all this talk about the giant dead black bird, and of course the fact that it was almost Halloween didn't help matters at all.

Cosmas had stopped listening after my words "dispose of the body," as he knew what I was really saying was that *he* had to dispose of the body, and was now doing a little gross-me-out jig.

This was when I reminded him that he couldn't just put it in the building trash alley in case one of our neighbors happened upon it and mentioned it to another neighbor until eventually it came out that it was Wendell who had slain the bird and his reputation of sweet, darling dog of the building would be forever shattered. What if people didn't want to pet him anymore? What if they decided they didn't want him in the building? I mean, he was going to be an angel for Halloween (I found this great little set of wings) for Christ's sake, and I didn't mean the angel of death.

I was now expecting Cosmas to tell me that I was crazy and that there was no way he was going to bury a dead bird, but he didn't. Instead he told me that we didn't have a shovel.

He had me there. We modern urbanites tend to take things like shovels for granted. It's just one of those things that everyone seems to have—like an Igloo water cooler. I wondered whether people register for shovels when they get married.

"Maybe you could borrow one?" I shrugged helplessly.

It was now Cosmas's turn to roll his eyes and make me feel stupid for a change.

"Okay, so I should just knock on our neighbor's door and

say hi, sorry to knock so late, but we were wondering whether you might have a shovel that we could use right now in the dark of night, and oh, by the way, if you happen to have a large tarp, that might be helpful, too. Ha! They'd be calling the police before I even had a chance to get back over here."

Another good point on his part, as I checked my watch and it was eleven-thirty, so there wasn't a real justification in terms of why exactly we'd need a shovel now, damn this New England weather, never a freak snowstorm when you need one.

Suddenly I stood up, hands on hips, determined—and said the two words that I knew would strike fear into Cosmas's heart. "Home Depot."

Cosmas cringed, and then shook his head. "No. You know how I feel about that place. I don't do Home Depot." Cosmas did not respond well to crowds, supersize stores, or anything that made him feel inadequate (let's just say Cosmas is not what you would call a handy guy).

I, myself, was a little intimidated by Home Depot as well, but at least my priorities were in place, so I was willing to sacrifice my own insecurities for the sake of my dog.

"Look, I think we're panicking here. Perhaps we should sit down and figure out a plan of action."

It was obvious Cosmas was stalling, but just then I realized that Home Depot would more than likely be closed and that our only hope was that I thought the Target near us might possibly be open twenty-four hours.

Next came the issue of where we would bury the bird, and

soon we were both scratching our heads over it. . . . Again, another problem with living in a metropolitan city, nowhere to bury dead bodies.

It was Cosmas who suggested the public gardens one street over, and I quickly agreed. There were at least a few plots that weren't being used and if we buried the bird deep enough I'm assuming it wouldn't hurt the plants, and besides, if it was a crow, perhaps it'd be more at peace knowing it was buried where you could grow corn.

As Cosmas and I were now dressed all in black, wearing rubber-soled shoes so we could go stealth, I started to really think about what we were actually willing to do for Wendell. Wendell was still asleep at the foot of our bed, probably—so sweet, so peaceful, so unaware of the lengths his parents were willing to go to for his reputation. I mean, now that I was thinking about the whole thing, it was rather preposterous, and who knew that we had it in us to be so devious. But, love was irrational, love was unconditional, and love was even at times dead big black birds.

Before we left to go buy a shovel I told Cosmas that I wanted to see the body. He told me to go ahead but that he would rather wait in the car (can you say *sissy?*), but when I got to the grassy patch I couldn't find it—no bird, not even a feather. At this my heart leapt with joy—joy that my dog was no longer a murderer (or at least couldn't be convicted in a court of law), joy that I now got to go and tell my husband we didn't have to be accomplices (or have to go to Target), and joy that we now had a spooky story to share for Halloween.

The 10 Breeds of Obsessed Dog Owners

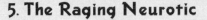

5. The Raging Neurotic

This dog owner has a high-pitched nervous laugh that bursts forth at odd times and is somewhat reminiscent of a jackal's. Always watching every move their dogs make, they can never look you in the eye, and they're constantly saying things like "No! Stop that! Don't eat that!" and "What's that you are eating?! What's in your mouth?! OHMYGOD WHAT'S IN YOUR MOUTH?!" And they generally seem on the verge of hysteria. They constantly change veterinarians and will get enraged if their vets don't return their calls promptly (though perhaps this is because it's the tenth time this month that they've called to discuss the fact that their dog's nose doesn't seem as cool and wet as it should be). They are constantly seeking the opinion of everyone around them regarding their dogs. "Do his eyes look a little red to you? Can dogs get pinkeye? Ohmygod, he's got pinkeye. I've got to call my vet." Their dogs always seem a bit sleepy, but this is probably because they get woken up a lot, as their owners are constantly afraid they are going to stop breathing in their sleep and die.

Do Your Dog's Haircuts Cost More Than Your Own?

DON'T CRY OVER CUT HAIR

Sure, there are more important things to get upset over in life than your dog's hair, and of course I know this, but somehow I just couldn't help myself. Because when it comes to dogs, what kind of public identity do they *have* besides their hair? I mean, sure there's breed, and personality, but let's just stick with the basics for a moment—hair is really a big deal for dogs; at least the ones who have good hair, anyway.

Wendell has good hair, so good, in fact, that it's the defining characteristic of his official dog breed, which is, and please note this, *soft coated* wheaten terrier. Now, if something like that is included in one's official title then it has to be true—sort of like someone being named Baroness something or other. His hair on a good day, when it's clean and conditioned (as opposed to when he's clean and conditioned but has been rolling around in those stupid propeller thingies that fall off trees in the summer—the ones that used to be so fun to play with when you were little but now you hate, as they get all over the sidewalks and produce some sticky pollen residue that dogs, especially my dog, loves to grind himself into [I call this move his Darling Nicki]), is incredibly silky and smooth. So darn soft that all you can do is say the hell with doing laundry, and instead sit on the couch with him by your side and rub on him all day long while watching bad movies on cable.

As far as the color, well, from afar it is "wheat" colored, but as you get closer you see that in actuality this honey/wheat color is an amalgamation of the finest blond strands of hair—like gossamer or angel thread (I just made that up, but it sounds nice, eh?), and coarser strands of a rusty red brown, and black, which all combine together. On a breezy day his hair floats and sways, moving like ballerinas pretending to be wheat on a windy day. If Wendell were human and female he'd be one of those women who appear on the TV commercials selling shampoo—shown in slow motion whipping around the most impossibly shiny silky bouncy hair ever. Now don't even get me started on what it feels like to run your fingers through it, but it's similar to the experience of that first bite of a chocolate-chip pancake after being on the Atkins diet for like forever (okay, three months).

Of course I don't love Wendell just for his hair, but on my shallow days I can gather a surprising amount of satisfaction from it. So of course when he starts to get too shaggy and frizzed out, or when he comes home with a bad haircut (looking either like those mean winged monkeys from *The Wizard of Oz* that I used to be scared of, or too short in the face *and* around the eyes, which makes them appear too dark and slightly menacing, and even worse is when they go too short around the eyes and then they leave his muzzle and chin hair too long and he sort of looks like a sketchy opium addict), I can't help but feel annoyed. I believe it all comes down to potential—meaning I know he has the potential to look like the cutest stuffed animal in the window of a toy store and I know that everyone on the street can't help but admire him, many even having to vocalize it by stopping me and saying things like "That hair. What great hair" (usually women, metrosexuals, or gay men), and depending on how demure I feel at the time I respond with a beaming, silent nod, or if I'm feeling a bit bolder I'll join in and say, "Thanks, isn't it just grand? What I would do for such hair." So of course when he's not living up to his hair potential I feel completely reasonable in being sulky.

Cosmas, of course, hates it when I criticize Wendell, and always jumps to his defense and I am immediately cast as Mommie Dearest one step away from Cruella de Vil (oh please, only a blonde would look really good in a coat of Wendell's hair).

"Stop calling him names," Cosmas calls out from the couch.

As he says this I roll my eyes, and debate whether to let it go or not. I decided not, since I was cranky over Wendell's Fu Manchu do. "I am not calling him names." This was technically true, as what I was doing was making screeching noises, flapping my arms, and chasing Wendell around the kitchen like he had pigtails and ruby slippers. (Wendell loved it, by the way.)

"Yeah, but you're making fun of him all the same." Cosmas has always been extremely sensitive about anyone getting made fun of. (Cosmas's favorite thing to do after elementary school was going to the library to read old issues of *Scientific American*, need I go on?)

"Oh please, he hasn't even seen *The Wizard of Oz*," I said, a little breathless and a lot dizzy, as Wendell ran around in circles when giddy with delight.

"I don't care that he's never seen the movie, the point is that I don't like you making fun of him. He looks fine."

"No, he doesn't look fine. He looks like a flying winged monkey." I flapped my arms again just to irritate him.

"Well, I don't see him flapping his arms around the room."

"Wings."

"What?"

"You said flapping his arms—it's wings."

"What?"

"WINGS! FLYING MONKEYS HAVE WINGS, NOT ARMS."

"Exactly." Cosmas threw his arms up in the air and shook his head like an exasperated pony. (This was a signature move, which I loved.)

It was my turn to say *what*. "What?"

"Wendell has arms, not wings." Yes, another case of Cosmas thinking of Wendell as human.

"Wendell has paws, not wings, or maybe it's legs. Paws are the equivalent of hands, right?" Now I was a little confused myself, and suddenly I had a grainy image in my head of Dorothy and Toto being carried off by the winged monkeys who actually seemed to have both arms and wings—oh well, can't be right all the time.

Cosmas yelled out "Stop it!" in the same way he yells at Wendell when he gets up and starts barking early in the morning at anything that sounds like dog tags (which is everyone who happens to park a car on our street). Then he gave me a pretty good imitation of my very own oh-no-you-don't-don't-give-me-that-look-like-you-don't-know-why-you're-in-trouble look, which stopped me cold in my tracks. I think I even hung my head a bit, as I, like Wendell, hated to get scolded.

I opened my mouth to speak out in my own defense, but Cosmas cut me off. "I don't want you to make fun of Wendell. It's not nice, and in fact it's mean."

My mouth popped open once again, but again Cosmas silenced me. "I don't care that he doesn't know what you're saying because he's a dog. I can hear what you're saying and I don't like it. Okay?"

I never go down without a fight and I was prepared to launch into a whole tirade about all the ways that I'm nice to Wendell, and I'm so far from being mean you'd have to put on sunglasses because it's daylight over there, but something stopped me. What stopped me was the fact that I decided that it was pretty endearing that Cosmas took on the role of Wendell's protector. Sure there were obviously some deep-rooted psychological issues at work here, but who cares about all that playground stuff from long ago, what was important now was that Cosmas loved Wendell enough to anthropomorphize him, which I felt was a very good thing.

This is when Wendell flipped his bowl over in the kitchen. This move was new to his repertoire, and it was something I hated. So bossy, so petulant, but yet I guess I'd be cranky, too, if I were thirsty. But really, why not a short bark? The flipping of the bowl was so bold, so violent (well, not violent as in AK-47s but a little brusque for a fuzzy lamb chop like himself), and was such a guy move that I wondered whether he was asserting his masculinity in some way. Of course Cosmas thought the flipping of the water bowl was hilarious. "That's m'boy." Oh, whatever.

I poured him water and watched him drink. No, I actually believe that Wendell realizes that part of his charm is his hair and of course he likes getting petted (I mean, who doesn't?), as there are plenty of times when he wants to sit in my lap and just get rubbed on.

No, the hair thing was definitely my issue, but oh well, who cares if I care about his hair? It's gorgeous and it's not like it's going anywhere.

🐾   🐾   🐾

I was crying over Wendell's hair, and I knew it was stupid, but I couldn't help it. I had been trying to cover up my tears for the last ten minutes, but I knew that I was doing a lousy job of it (clearing your throat, muffled sniffly sighs, and fluffing up your pillows with a little more pounding than necessary are not subtle signs). Of course I knew that Cosmas knew that I was crying and was now probably going down a checklist in his head, trying to figure out whether he was somehow involved, and if so, whether I'd believe he was actually asleep despite the fact that I was now basically snoring while awake with a nose full of mucus. Yucko.

Finally, he moved in and tried the silent approach of stroking my hair, hoping that was all he'd have to do—a little there-there-honey-I-feel-your-pain-and-sometimes-it-really-*doesn't*-help-to-talk-about-what's-upsetting-you-sometimes-all-you-need-is-a-good-night-of-sleep-to-feel-all-better-and-oh-by-the-way-did-I-mention-that-I-have-to-go-in-to-work-really-early-tomorrow-morning? Before I had a chance to dash all hope of an easy out, Wendell rolled on his back at the foot of the bed and did that thing where he slept with his four legs sticking straight up in the air (I loved when he did the dead-dog pose, so damn cute) and a tiny bit of light crept into the dark bedroom (too lazy to turn off the kitchen light) and shined right on his four outstretched legs. Normally, this was the point where I'd sigh, filled with love at the way his gorgeous blond hair flowed off his skinny legs, but not this time. This time, my wet, bleary eyes were drawn to the fact that his two back legs were shaved down to the skin, bare like a chicken leg after Super Bowl Sunday, and only the front two legs were in the proper glorious state (though the front right leg had a little shaved patch in the center like a poodle's, where the IV had been, but I couldn't see it at the moment by how he lay).

We had recently suffered through a rather traumatic few weeks where Wendell had come down with a mysterious fever, and had been sick as a dog (I mean this figuratively, and of course, literally) until we found out that he had a horribly huge abscess in his right hind leg. He ended up in the hospital for four nights, with six little incisions in his leg to drain out the pus (looked even worse than it sounds), and the left leg got shaved down because of all the yucky stuff that kept draining all over it. The whole thing had been an incredibly draining (pun intended) experience, first emotionally, and secondly to our bank account (two thousand smackeroos, I kid you not). Luckily, he was now on the mend with black stitches in his leg, and an appetite for being spoiled with scrambled eggs and Campbell's Chunky Chicken Noodle soup.

Due to his hospital stay, the fact that my husband had to carry Wendell's forty-five-pound frame up and down our apartment stairs three times a day, and the fact that I was unfortunately out of town on business, the rest of Wendell's coat was now a mess. Wendell's hair matted incredibly easily, and without his normal shampoo and deep-conditioning cream rinse and his daily combing, he was a total mess. First off, I'm loath to admit, he sort of smelled (though I was blaming his gross leaky wound; keep in mind that bacteria really stinks), secondly, he was sort of greasy-stringy-looking (the big plastic funnel collar on his head didn't help, either), and the tangles, oy, he was one day away from Milli Vanilli white

dog rapper Rastafarian (Milli Vanilli, because obviously
Wendell can't really sing, either).

Everyone I consulted said it would be better if we just
shaved him down to let all his hair grow back in together, and
even though I nodded in agreement as they told me this, in-
side I was screaming *NO, NO, ANYTHING BUT THAT!
DO YOU KNOW HOW LONG IT'S TAKEN TO GET HIS
HAIR TO LOOK THIS GOOD? HOW MANY HOURS OF
COMBING I'VE DONE? ALL THOSE DAYS OF TRIM-
MING SPLIT ENDS BY HAND? THAT TIME I SPENT
THREE HOURS GETTING OUT SOME RANDOM PER-
SON'S GUM THAT HE ROLLED IN? THAT'S IT? JUST
CUT IT ALL OFF?*

My biggest irrational fear (I had many) was that perhaps
Wendell was a reincarnated Samson and all his strength and
mythical presence was somehow wrapped up in his mane. Was
I to be the evil, calculating, heartless Delilah who just chopped
it all off, robbing him of his entire identity? In my head I
watched a buck-naked Wendell-phoenix rising up out of the
mounds of fallen fur (which looked like ashes, of course, for
the phoenix reference to work) to stand for just a moment,
only to collapse in a dramatic sigh back onto the floor, dead.

With this thought I bolted up straight in bed with a
shriek, which caused Cosmas to bolt up and away from me in
fear, and Wendell to be up on all fours in a flash, barking and
growling like Cujo on a bad day. Now I was sobbing and
shaking in total abandon. Now Cosmas realized that his
hair-rubbing didn't really work. He squinted at my wet,

snotty face, probably thankful that it was dark in the room since I was pretty horrific-looking as it was, and God help him if he was forced to turn on the light.

"Is something wrong?" he asked.

Ahhh, leave it to the sleepy, bewildered husband to come up with the one line that would make me even cry harder than I already was. WAS SOMETHING WRONG? WAS SOMETHING WRONG? OF COURSE SOME-THING WAS WRONG, OR IT WOULDN'T SEEM LIKELY THAT I WAS MUCKING UP THE VERY SHEETS THAT I HAD JUST CHANGED THAT VERY MORNING (I hated doing laundry, so clean sheets were a reason to celebrate in our household).

Wendell had now realized that we were not under attack and that it was just me, his mommy, throwing a fit (I wonder, since he's a boy dog, whether he knew what PMS was) and had settled back down into the comforter and was watching us both suspiciously, hoping that perhaps I'd get up to go and get some vanilla ice cream (his favorite) to drown away my human sorrows.

Finally, after a few minutes of more nose blowing and the-atrics on my part (the old back-of-the-hand-across-the-fore-head of woe is me with a combo *Home Alone* face-slap shriek), I started to settle down. In a being-chased-by-Pepé-Le-Pew voice I panted out my concerns of Wendell's pending haircut. I tried to calculate the number of hours I had spent on his coat since we had gotten him a year ago, but I soon lost track (I was never very good at math and multiplying in my head).

Cosmas's expression was hard to read, as there was a mixture of relief that it wasn't his neck on the chopping block and dismay that he wasn't sure how to handle my newest irrational fixation. He first tried the medical approach by telling me that no one in the history of man (and dog) had ever died by having their hair cut (minus some freak razor accident that he still doubted could kill a person). Next he explained the physiological nature of hair growth and the fact that hair is continually growing, so Wendell's coat would be back to its normal glory within a few weeks.

I arched my eyebrow in response until he amended his answer to months, then several months, to less than a year. I reminded him that in dog years one year was seven, and that Wendell would have to suffer through his teen years with one bad-hair day after another. At this new thought, I wondered if anyone made wigs for dogs? What about some sort of hair extension for his back legs? What about Rogaine, would that speed up the whole process? I moved across the bed, refusing to let our sleeping dog lie, and began to run my fingers through his tangled hair.

Cosmas, now cranky and wanting to go back to sleep, asked the tough question. "So is it Wendell's image and well-being that you're worried about or your own?"

Ouch. I opened my mouth to respond, but promptly closed it because I didn't know what to say. I tried again—nothing. I thought about the fact that originally I had wanted a French bulldog instead of a wheaten terrier because I had seen this woman in Grand Central Station once who was all glammed out standing next to a huge pile of Louis Vuitton luggage with a little white French bulldog sitting on the top of the pile. How that image has stayed with me for years, and how I thought the dog was the best accessory I had ever seen. I thought about the fact that I enjoyed how cute Wendell was as we walked about Cambridge. How the women at the Saks shoe department raved over him when we were there last fall (one salesperson even asked whether I had highlighted his hair; as if).

The third time I opened my mouth to respond with no answer that I cared to say out loud, I faked a pretty realistic yawn, fluffed my pillows gently, and then quickly flopped down in bed and assumed a sleep position. I heard Cosmas sigh, and then he quietly got back into bed with his back pressed up against my own. I listened as his breath began to slow, and soon it played back up with Wendell's own breathing rhythm—yes, both my boys were now fast asleep. I yawned for real, and shut my eyes. My last thought was wondering what size Ziploc bag I would need to hold all of Wendell's hair, which I would gather up after it had been shorn, because if I couldn't find someone who knew how to make body toupees for dogs, then surely I'd find someone who could make me a little furry accessory (a scarf, hat, or perhaps a little throw rug). As of tomorrow I was excusing Wendell from that job.

The Do's and Don'ts of Shopping for an Obsessed Dog Owner

DO know that all obsessed dog owners are very discriminating when it comes to toys and treats for their dog, so anything you buy for the dog must be carefully researched and considered.

DO assume that the dog has a signature color (and perhaps even a palette of choice). This color of choice can oftentimes be determined by his flat collar and lead, but know that he may have several. (Also note that even if a dog's signature color is red, it might be a specific red, as in blue-red, and not orange-red.)

DO think carefully when it comes to doggy treats, as most owners are very strict when it comes to their dog's diet. (They can give their dog junk food, but won't think kindly if you bring their dog junk food.)

DO take into consideration the size of the dog that you are purchasing a gift for—big dogs play with big toys and small dogs play with small toys. When it comes to medium-size dogs it is better to go bigger over smaller, as medium-size dogs sometimes have complexes and prefer to think of themselves as big dogs, and small toys may offend them.

DON'T automatically assume that the obsessed dog owner who you are shopping for will appreciate dog products featuring breeds of dogs other than her own. The owners of say, a soft coated wheaten terrier might not appreciate a wall calendar featuring Labradors (probably as she doesn't want to make her own dog jealous).

DON'T automatically assume that just because someone sells a sweatshirt that has a silk-screened picture of a wheaten terrier featured in a heart with the caption "I Love My Wheaten" that the owner of a wheaten will wear such a thing (well, unless the picture happens to be an actual photo of her dog—*that* she might wear).

DON'T feel that giving a dog cash or a gift certificate is an impersonal gift. Truth be told, the obsessed owner and the dog would probably be happier picking out their own presents than having to pretend that they like whatever it is you got them. 🐾

THE ART OF LOVE

Like most obsessive dog owners, I am a bit of a maniac when it comes to taking pictures of Wendell. And though I have a mammoth photo album of his entire life (he's two and a half), which I thrust into the hands of anyone who happens to step foot in our apartment, I still am proud to say that I'm not the type of crazy dog owner who has hundreds of framed pictures of her dog all over her apartment. In fact, I only have one puppy picture on my desk; okay, I have two (but Wendell was a really cute puppy). I have the few requisite action shots on the fridge, and I carry a Kate Spade leather travel picture frame in my purse (to thrust into the hands of those who won't have the luxury of getting to see his entire album), but that's about it. Okay, okay, I have a picture on my dresser, too, but who's counting?

The point is that even though I get the pleasure of having the real thing actually trotting about the house all day, I somehow wanted something *more*—a larger testament to show not only how important he was in my life, but also how special he really was. I wanted something that people would see and think, *Wow, what a dog,* or *Wow, this is a woman who truly appreciates her dog,* but something that wasn't so over-the-top as to cause a person to barely be able to make it down the front stairs of my building before she would burst out laughing at my expense.

"So, what you're basically saying is that you want a *shrine* to our dog, is that what I'm hearing?" Cosmas, my husband, said from the protection of the business section of *The New York Times*. He was half joking, but I detected a hint of jealousy.

I rolled my eyes even though he couldn't see me. "No one said anything about a shrine, I'm talking about something more along the lines of a . . ." I paused, looking for the right word.

"A memento?" He peeked over the paper and smiled.

"No, but close. I was thinking more along the lines of monumental. Yes, a monument to Wendell. I know, what about a bust?! Do people still get busts made?"

Cosmas crumpled his paper down so he could see if I was actually being serious.

I made a face to show him I was joking, but in actuality I was damning the fact that we didn't have room for a grand piano in our living room. Okay, no bust, but what about a nice piece of sculpture? Something made out of marble or granite. I hmmm, sculpture is sorta tricky, and you'd have to be pretty talented to convey warmth in stone. Though Wendell was at times almost brazenly independent, he also radiated inner warmth as well.

Then it came to me, why not a portrait? Something modern, yet classic, something bold, but not stuffy (because Wendell was not a stuffy dog), something warm, yet not overly cutesy. Now of course I'd have to find someone to paint him, and not just anybody. What I needed was someone who was *not* the typical pet-painter type (not that I knew what that type *was*, exactly, but I assumed it was probably along the lines of a little old lady who enjoys taking adult-education art classes). No, I needed someone who was a real hard-core artist, someone angry and temperamental who could only find relief from the demons in his head by painting or cutting off a body part (obviously his own body part and not that of his subject). I didn't share my revelation with Cosmas, as he was still snickering over the bust, but I didn't care; I now knew what I wanted.

🐾   🐾   🐾

I found the flyer in a small gallery on Newbury Street that showcased the paintings of new artists in the Boston area. The flyer showed three different paintings of dogs with a simple heading of "Paintings by Petersen Thomas" and at the bottom it said, "To commission a portrait of your pet, please contact . . ." I very casually picked one up and stared at it, not quite able to believe my good fortune, but my excitement grew as I studied the work. One painting in particular was especially fabulous; it featured a black Lab holding a bright green chew toy in its mouth against a shocking-pink background. It was bold, visually arresting, and modern.

I was with my friend Kyle at the time. Kyle recently bought a piano key that was painted with a female unicorn in the act of urinating for a few thousand dollars at an auction. So when he came over to see what I was staring at, I quickly tried to fold up the paper before he could get a glimpse of it.

"Whatcha got there?" he asked. At first I was reluctant to show it to him, because I doubted that he'd consider a pet painting to be much in the way of high art. But then I realized I did need a second opinion on whether this guy had any talent.

He studied it for a while and soon nodded his approval but warned me that portraits were tricky, because when it came right down to it, having someone capture the "essence" of a person, or in my case, a dog, was incredibly difficult, because beauty was subjective.

I carefully tucked the flyer in my purse and didn't respond, because maybe beauty was subjective, but as far as I was concerned, Wendell's looks were not.

🐾   🐾   🐾

I'm not exactly sure why I was nervous about calling the number on the flyer, but I was. As much as I considered myself arty, I was only arty in the sense that my friends and I read The New Yorker, saw the less indie films of the indie-film circuit (skipping over the ones that were either about wildlife or simply too depressing), read a lot of magazines, and wore a lot of black, but we were not arty in the sense of true artiness—like we were not painters, sculptors, or performance artists who would rather starve than sell out. (The only thing we might consider starving for was new shoes or a handbag.) But, at the same time, I did think it would be cool to have an arty friend or two.

Finally, I called. The voice that answered was surprisingly deep and robust, and fairly normal. I was sort of half expecting to hear the torture in his voice—"Christ! I don't paint by numbers!"—and that he would be a little surly. Painters in movies always seemed a bit brooding and surly, which I figured was just an attitude that they acquired from sitting in small dive bars where they sat around with other painters and nursed the one highball of booze they could afford at the moment, but maybe it had more to do with all the turpentine.

So I explained to him how I'd found his flyer, how I loved the pink Labrador painting, and that I was interested in speaking with him about a possible portrait of my dog, Wendell. I asked him how the "process" worked—meaning did he expect Wendell to sit for him, how much it cost, and whether or not I had any say-so at all. I was a little awkward on the phone, because of course I didn't want to step on his painter toes by being a neurotic and demanding client, but at the same time I already had a sense of what I wanted and was wondering what the polite way was to ask whether he'd be willing to set aside his artistic integrity for the whims of a slightly obsessive (or high-strung) dog owner. I mean, I had to assume he was used to such questions, because he obviously had painted a bunch of dogs already, and the type of dog owners that would actually commission portraits of their dogs all had to be somewhat similar—meaning they all had to be a bit obsessive when it came to their dogs.

He took all my questions in stride, and told me that he painted from pictures, but that he did like to meet the dogs as well. This immediately made me feel better, because honestly, what real painter wouldn't want to meet his subject? Even though I had some really amazing pictures of Wendell (he's quite photogenic), I was skeptical about whether an artist could capture his true essence—his intelligence, spirit, charm, and independence—without meeting him first.

After we set up a meeting at the Boston Common for the following week, I finally had enough nerve to ask him what I really wanted to know (I had thought about just asking him in person, but I figured it was easier to take a stranger laughing at you over the phone than face to face).

"So, uh, I, uh . . ." Nervousness always enhanced my eloquence. . . . "I was wondering how open you were to, say, well, you know, um . . . direction from your clients."

He paused, probably steeling himself for yet another inane question from a nonarty person, and then he spoke in a direct but polite voice: "I'm not sure I know what you mean."

Well, at least he was perceptive, because obviously I didn't, either. I tried again. "It's just that I know you're an artist, and I'm sure you might not be thrilled to have someone tell you how to paint, er, not that I would ever tell you how to paint, that's not what I mean." I took a deep breath. "What I'm trying to say is that I don't have an exact picture of Wendell that I like, and I wanted to know whether you'd be able to sort of improvise a little, I mean, of course you must improvise all the time, and I certainly don't mean to say that you don't have imagination, because I'm sure you do, but what I mean is that I sort of have an idea of what I'd like and I was wondering whether you'd be open to hearing a suggestion. But at the same time I don't want to offend you because I'm pretty sure that Wendell would be a muse for anyone, but—"

Finally he took pity and interrupted me. This I liked,

because it showed him to be impatient, yet empathetic at the same time. (I mean, weren't artists *all* about contradictions?)

"Well, if you're asking me whether or not I'd be open to suggestions when it comes to the dog portraits, absolutely. Some of my clients have asked for a specific background color or to change the color of the couch so it matched their living room; it's no problem. Right now I'm doing pet portraits on the side of my other painting. When it comes to other work, no, I wouldn't really be interested in direction. So, what do you have in mind?"

I'd love to know right then what he was thinking I was going to ask because I'm pretty sure that there was no way he would have ever imagined that I was going to ask what I asked. "I was hoping that you might consider doing Wendell's portrait in a similar style to Picasso's Blue Period."

Long silence.

I continued talking fast with excitement because the thought of it really did make me giddy with delight, I mean, how fabulous would that look?! "I don't mean to say you can't add in your own style, whatever that may be, but after you see Wendell I think you'll agree that he's really worthy of something along those lines. He has such a gorgeous coat that is actually made up of varying colors of white, blond, red, and black, which in combination gives him his wheaten color."

More silence.

Finally, he spoke, his voice pretty soft now. "Are you serious?"

Hmmm, that's a toughie, because I actually was serious,

and now I had to determine whether he was pissed *and* incredulous, or just incredulous.

"I am. I just have this picture in my head of it, and I think it'd be amazing. But of course when I say Picasso, I'm not really wanting Wendell to look depressed, or too serious, and not to mix Picasso periods, I'm definitely not interested in any subtle cubist context—no noses or guitars or misshapen heads." Artists were probably cringing in their graves all over Europe. . . .

Now it was Petersen's turn to stammer a bit. "I, uh, well, sure. I mean, I'd be willing to try it out. I actually think I'm pretty good with figuring out the styles of the greats. It'd certainly be an interesting project. Very, uh . . ."

I piped in, trying to be helpful. "Bold? Daring? What I'm really looking for is something that is sort of, oh, you know—monumental."

"Absolutely" was his response, and I wondered whether it was *absolutely I'll try because hey, we artist types take risks and are all about monumental, or absolutely—like as soon as I get off the phone I'm absolutely going to change my phone number, you wack job.*

And so it began.

🐾 🐾 🐾

When I received Petersen's call two weeks later asking whether I had time to come over to see his "first draft" I immediately agreed to come over that very day, but after I hung up the phone I found myself suddenly nervous. What if I hated it? What if it looked nothing like Wendell? What if he totally didn't "get" Wendell's essence? Was I crazy to have even suggested the whole "blue" thing in the first place, maybe Wendell wasn't the Blue Period type; after all, didn't I always put him in collars that were red?

I thought back to the day before Petersen first met Wendell, how I spent the entire afternoon in the library poring over art books just to make sure there wasn't another "style" that might better represent Wendell's look. I covered all the bases—Degas (too many ballerinas, Wendell was very masculine), Chagall (too whimsical), Miró (too many straight lines, Wendell's hair was wavy), Monet (too soft-focus), Dalí (too melty bizarre), Munch (too alarmist), Renoir (too cliché), Lichtenstein (too many dots), Basquiat (too crackhouse gritty), Warhol (too overexposed), Pollock (too messy), O'Keeffe (too vaginal), Kahlo (too many skulls and, I'm sorry, but I still don't get the unibrow thing)—but in the end I realized that I had made the right selection in the beginning. Picasso was perfect—daring, confident, lots of attitude, a little dark, but not in a fake way, and with just enough mystery to make it interesting. . . .

Petersen's studio was in his apartment, which happened to be at the very top of Beacon Hill in Boston, and as I trudged up the hill I tried to get into the right frame of mind. I reminded myself that no matter how it turned out, especially if I didn't like it, I needed to maintain my composure. Petersen happened to be a pretty big guy (over six feet and at least 250 pounds), and though I doubted he'd be the type to start throwing things and breaking chairs, I still didn't want to hurt his feelings.

When he walked me into his studio, I was holding my breath, so when I saw the painting, I gasped. It was even better than the one I had imagined, and I loved it immediately, but there was one slight problem—Wendell's face. Though there was no doubt that it *was* a wheaten terrier, I have to say that the face was just a tiny bit off from being Wendell, though perhaps some might think it could be a relative of his. Petersen could tell that something was amiss and explained again that this was just the first draft and the whole point of doing the painting in two stages was that it would give me a chance to make changes. That was all the encouragement I needed, and soon I was standing behind him as he worked directly on the painting   eyes a little farther apart, hair a little more tousled (think of lone breeze in desert), the hair around his mouth was probably a bit darker, and his face was a little too long. After only a few minutes of brush strokes, suddenly the painting was transformed (before my very eyes) into my darling Wendell. With my hand over my mouth, I whispered, "That's it. That's Wendell."

I picked up the final a week later, and it was even better. The painting was everything I had hoped—a monument, a piece of art, and it looked just like Wendell, but in blue.

The 10 Breeds of Obsessed Dog Owners

6. The "My Dog, My Accessory" Owner

These owners usually tend to have those little dogs that sort of look like those pom-pom things at the ends of pencils—you know, the ones that you twirl between your palms and then the pom-pom thingies get all poofed out? These owners' dogs are always immaculately groomed and have more than one collar and matching leads. These dogs are sort of like Barbie dolls in a way and have more outfits, more hair doodads, and better bedding than you do. These owners are always fussing with their dog's designer raincoats, showing you how they actually replaced the original buttons with baby blue buttons that perfectly match their dog's baby blue collar—the same collar that perfectly brings out the blue of their blue-black coat of hair. This is when you notice that the dog's hair is quite silky-smooth and very shiny. This is when you think of your own hair and the fact that perhaps you should find out what salon she goes to, as her hair is so much nicer than your own, and then you notice that the diamonds on her choker are bigger than the ones on your own wedding ring and you feel a little bit bad about yourself. . . .

Does Your Dog Get More Heavy Petting Than Your Significant Other?

CRINKY CRANKY JEALOUS

Cosmas and I were in a doozy of a fight, and I was in that state of mind where if I were in a movie I'd pack up my matching suitcases, put on a hat that ties under the chin with a ribbon (one that is the exact color of my high-heeled T-straps), and would march out the door without so much as a backward glance to go and stay with my mother. But of course this would never happen, as I don't have matching suitcases, I don't wear hats—well, I do, but I hardly think a Lacoste bucket hat is the sort of look I'd be going for at the moment, and if I left Cosmas I could never go and stay with my mother, as she'd probably shoot me on sight if she knew I left him. (Mom loves Cosmas.) So instead I was standing in front of an open freezer staring at a couple bags of frozen mixed vegetables (why I buy them, I don't know. I never use them, and yet I keep buying them. It must be an aspirational thing, like I wish I were the type of person to eat frozen vegetables, hell, or vegetables in general. Sometimes I think that I should throw them out, but I never do, thinking that if someone got punched in the face it would be helpful to have some frozen peas to help stop the swelling). I had been standing there for at least five minutes trying to conjure up a pint of Ben & Jerry's ice cream.

I closed my eyes, and scrunched up my forehead, and sighed, blowing my hair out of my face. "Dammit, where's that Harry Potter kid when you need him?" And I shut the freezer. "Yes, that's what I need, a boy magician—able to make ice cream appear and husbands disappear." I cackled a tad unattractively at this, and on cue Wendell came trotting into the room, nails clicking, with an expression of pure rapture.

"Ooops, sorry bunbun, I shouldn't have said the I-word." And I gave his furry head a little rub.

He was now sitting at my feet, having totally ignored my apology, and I was a bit unnerved at his unblinking gaze. *You said ice cream. I want ice cream.*

Just then Wendell did that thing where he let his back legs slide out from under him so he was now lying down at my feet. *Fine, if you want to play hardball, that's fine by me.* His back haunches were pretty tight, as he was ready to spring at any second if I happened to reach for a container that looked like it might contain ice cream. I closed the freezer door and said, "See?"

Still no blink, so I guess the gesture was lost on him.

Trying again, I opened the freezer back up and waved my

hand before it in order to show my dog, who stood only twenty inches tall, that if he could stand upright and peer into the freezer himself he would see that there was no ice cream to be found.

"Frozen vegetables," I said, grabbing a bag and waving it at him. "Yucko."

He was in sit position again, his head cocked to the left. *Ice cream now comes in bags? What will they think of next?*

I shook my head and answered my dog's questioning stare (hey, I didn't sleep well, cut me some slack, okay?). "This is not *you know what*, this is frozen vegetables."

Head now cocked to the right. *Maybe you are just showing me the frozen vegetables as a decoy move so that you can really save all the ice cream for yourself.*

I was offended that he would even think such a thing, so in one fell swoop I squatted down and picked him up in my arms (ooof, either I need to work out more, or he needs to stop eating ice cream), so that he was now eye level with the open freezer and could see for himself. "See. No ice cream."

At the mention of the I-word he started to struggle and for a moment I almost lost my grip and then *thwack*, I got a paw right in my eye. Somehow I managed to get him back on the floor upright, where he immediately started to bark at me. "Bark bark bark." *Now. Now. Now.*

Ordinarily I'd be pretty annoyed at his audacity, as I did not raise him to be a bratty dog, but not today. Today I was in a bad mood. Today I didn't feel like imparting a lesson on him to say that bratty dogs don't get ice cream. Today I was in need of a little ice cream myself, so I said, "Fine, you win. Let's go for a car ride."

Ten minutes later we were sitting at a small table in front of Wendell's favorite ice-cream shop in Harvard Square, Toscanini's, me with one scoop of Hydrox cookie in a sugar cone, and Wendell with a small cup of strawberry. Me with my elbows on the table and my chin in one hand, him by my chair next to me walking around in circles as he scooted his cup around on the sidewalk. Normally I'd do that friendly-smile-and-nod thing as the passersby pointed and exclaimed over Wendell and his ice cream (is it really so weird to give a dog his own ice cream? I mean, it's not like we were sharing a cone or anything). No, today, I'm pissed at Cosmas and couldn't care less if people think it's cute or strange or funny that I would give my dog his own ice cream, especially at ten in the morning. Besides, if I had the power to make my dog happy, then why shouldn't I?

I mean, it made sense that sometimes we needed to see physical proof of love in relationships, whether it be ice cream in the morning, or something small like NOT LEAVING YOUR WIFE ON THE COUCH ASLEEP ALL NIGHT SO THAT SHE WAKES UP WITH A CRINK IN HER NECK AND THEN DISCOVERS THAT HER HUSBAND, THE LOVE OF HER LIFE, ACTUALLY TOOK THE TIME TO CARRY THEIR SLEEPING DOG TO BED WITH HIM BUT THEN FORGOT ALL ABOUT HIS WIFE. I MEAN, COME ON! AND WHEN CONFRONTED BY HIS WIFE

WITH THE CRINKED-UP NECK THE NEXT
MORNING ALL HE COULD SAY WAS THAT HE
WAS HALF ASLEEP HIMSELF AND THAT HE
FORGOT. AND WHEN CONFRONTED AGAIN BY
HIS WIFE, WHO ASKED THEN WHY DIDN'T HE
FORGET TO BRING THE DOG TO BED, TOO, HE
REPLIED THAT THE DOG WAS SOFT AND NOT
AS HEAVY AS THE WIFE. CAN YOU BELIEVE
THAT? WHAT MAN IN HIS RIGHT MIND
WOULD CALL HIS WIFE FAT AND ROUGH-
SKINNED TO HER FACE, ESPECIALLY WHEN
HER NECK WAS SORE?!!

This is when I look over at Wendell and see that he is
now chewing the cup, hoping to squeeze out all remnants of
strawberry flavor from the cardboard pulp. I gently pry open
his steel-trap mouth and take out what's left of the cup and I
tell him that I love him and then I try to rub his ears but he
pulls away from me and is now sniffing around the ground
looking for melted ice-cream drops to lick up off the dirty
ground. I try to discourage this by placing my flip-flop over a
few droplets but now he has his nose at the edge of my shoe
and is waiting for me to lift my foot. *I can play the waiting game,
too, lady, all I've got is time.* So I say, "No, Wendell. The ground
is dirty. No lick. Yucko. Ice cream is all gone. No ice cream."

At the words *ice cream* Wendell has now lifted his head
and promptly sits before me. *Did you say ice cream? I love ice
cream. Can I have some ice cream?*

This sort of frustrates me as obviously he just had some ice cream and I don't understand why he can't just be happy over that. Why must he always want more? Why can't he ever be satisfied? I shake my head no. "No more." This is when he tries to slide out his back legs into down position, but it's not easy on the sidewalk, so he flops down the regular way and is soon looking up at me. *Please. Please. Please.* (Can you say déjà vu?)

"Look, Wendell, you just had a whole thing of ice cream and you should just be happy with what you've had. We can't have everything, right?"

He whines. *Pretty please.*

"Don't beg, Wendell, it's tacky."

Wendell, not wanting to be tacky, or probably more likely deciding that I'm just plain mean, gave up and was now lying down next to me, facing away (which is what he does when he's icing me out).

This was when I started to zone out and engaged in my normal runaway fantasy of living in Mexico at a small hotel by the ocean where I could be the waitress at a bar on the beach (one that wasn't busy, as who wants to work a lot in a fantasy), where a lot of interesting fugitives would show up and entertain me with stories of their bank heists and how they almost got caught, but managed to escape and just left their old lives behind. And there was always one guy who had lots of cool scars who drank scotch at 10:00 A.M. after his walk on the beach and I would ask him whether he missed his old life, and he'd say not really, and then he'd get a soulful look on his face, and I'd busy myself wiping down the bar, giving him time to collect his thoughts, as it's obvious that he wanted to tell me something, and then he'd look out into the dazzling ocean and just sigh. This is when I would give him a free shot, and he'd look over at me and say that the only thing he missed was the dog, Chivas, which he had to leave behind.

Suddenly my reverie ended and it occurred to me that I hadn't had a flight fantasy since we had gotten Wendell, and of course I would never leave Wendell behind. (Wendell would also hate Mexico, as he doesn't like direct sunlight if the temperature is over eighty-five degrees, and of course the beach was a no-go in general, as his fine hair was a sand magnet.)

It was then that my mobile phone rang and I picked it up and stared at the caller ID blinking "Husband" at me. Right as I was about to hit "talk" to answer the phone I gave myself a stern little warning. "Be calm. You have ice cream." When I answered I tried to do it in a tone that I knew would force him to squirm a bit—meaning that I didn't sound totally pissed, but I didn't sound totally happy to hear from him either. I was sort of going for the tone that would convey that I was in a travel agent's office looking through suddenly-single cruise brochures. (Men must be kept on their toes at all times.)

Needing more to go on than my one-note "Hi," Cosmas said, "Whatcha doing?"

"Just hanging out wondering whether Wendell would like living out west." Petty, I know, but it takes a passive-aggressive to know one.

"What happened to Mexico?"

I couldn't help but smile at the fact that Cosmas remembered my runaway-fantasy locale (as what's the point of running away if your husband doesn't know where to come and find you so he can beg for forgiveness and give you lots of diamonds?). "I don't think Wendell would have much fun hanging out with a bunch of Chihuahuas."

Cosmas sighed, as he now had an effective reading of where I was on the snarky scale. (I was at four on the ten-point scale—sarcasm with intent to be annoying.) "I see."

"Really, do you? Like the way you saw that half the bed was empty, since your wife was nowhere to be found? I mean, what if I had been kidnapped?" Oh well, so much for keeping calm. And with that I started World War III, and next thing you know he was asking if that's the way I wanted to play and I heard myself saying yeah, and that his battleship was almost sunk, "and furthermore, just so everything is clear, I want you to know that Wendell goes with me." Snarky meter was now at nine—melodramatic grandstanding worthy of an Aaron Spelling show.

Our call ended shortly thereafter, and five minutes later I was eating a scoop of toasted coconut with a side of chocolate sprinkles (I like putting them on myself) and Wendell got a half scoop of banana.

Later that night when Cosmas and I were ignoring each other while watching *Friends*, both of us sitting as far away from each other as you can on a five-foot couch, I noticed Wendell sitting in his chair looking far sulkier than a dog who got two cups of ice cream in one day should look. I wondered whether he knew we were fighting, and was now scared that he'd end up being shuttled around between two homes on every other weekend and major holidays.

As an experiment I moved my feet from the coffee table and swung them ninety degrees and into Cosmas's lap. Cosmas, who was now more mad at me than I was at him (my anger is like a flash flood—quick and over before you know it), looked at my feet with disdain but didn't push them away.

I then mouthed "Rub my feet" to Cosmas and did a few head jerks in Wendell's direction.

Cosmas, not understanding the whole point of mouthing something, replied, "I'm not going to rub your feet. I'm still mad at you."

I rolled my eyes and tried to explain that I wasn't asking him to rub my feet for my own sake (geez, how selfish did he think I was?) but that I was asking him to do it for Wendell's sake.

I watched as Cosmas tried to make sense of this, but couldn't quite put it together and was also suspicious that I was just trying to trick him into giving me a foot massage.

Finally I had to spell the whole thing out for him.

Cosmas shook his head to show that he thought I was full of it, but as I watched him study Wendell, who had raised his chin off his paws and was staring at us with his big, liquid, puppy-dog eyes, I saw Cosmas's expression soften and then he began to rub my feet.

Wendell still looked doubtful, so I bailed on the foot

massage and scooted over so I was right next to Cosmas and was now resting my face on his chest. I even made a few sound effects: *Mmmmmmmmmm.* Finally Wendell put his head back down and then soon closed his eyes. Ah-ha. It worked. Just as I was about to pop back up like a jack-in-the-box, Cosmas put his arms around me and murmured, "Not so fast, you." Wow, Cosmas really did have a sexy raspy voice when he wanted to use it.

I looked up at him, batting my eyelashes, and waited for him to give me a big smoldering movie kiss, but instead I got a lecture. (So not fair, entrapment by sexy voice!) In my lecture he told me that he could take my hysterical grandstanding about him not loving me enough to bring me to bed with him, and that he even found it sort of cute that I was actually jealous that he brought our dog to bed and forgot about me when he had been jealous for months and months over how much I kissed and cooed at our dog all the time when he had been left high and dry (oh please, I was not jealous of Cosmas's love for Wendell . . . okay, maybe just a little), and he could even take my sarcastic jokes about runaway fantasies whenever we were in a fight, but what he could not take and would not take were jokes about us splitting up and Wendell going with me. He said that he was really hurt by my earlier comment (so hurt that he stopped and got an ice-cream cone for himself after work and yes, he brought home a pint for me and Wendell, too—score!) and that after I hung up on him and he thought about a life devoid of a loudmouth wife and darling dog he realized that though his life would surely be a bit more peaceful it was also a life that he knew he never wanted, and that next time he was ever in a position similar to last night's (bleary-eyed and half asleep), he'd make damn sure that at least my neck was properly supported on the couch before he carried Wendell to bed.

Hardy. Hardy. Har-har. (Normally I would take great pride in the fact that Cosmas's ability to be funny had showed vast improvement since we married, but it's a bit harder to take when you're the butt of the joke.) But, not wanting to be one of those people who could dish it out but couldn't take it, I accepted his little funny ha-ha with a big smile instead, though truth be told I was more happy with the fact that he had just referred to me and Wendell as his family, and I thought that was like the cutest thing ever, well, after our sleeping dog.

Right then I noticed that Wendell was not actually asleep anymore but was looking at us quite smugly. *You guys are Play-Doh in my paws.* I smiled back at him and then turned back to Cosmas, where I pushed aside passiveness and aggressively gave him a big smoldering kiss.

NOT JUST A DOG

I can always tell when Cosmas comes home from work, before he ever walks through our door. Well, perhaps I should give credit where credit is due, and say that I am only privy to such knowledge because it is Wendell who lets me know. I would like to believe Wendell knows this because he has doggy ESP (but I've actually done a few "tests" and although Wendell has scored above average, he's no Nostradamus), but more realistically I think Wendell hears the distinctive beep that our car makes when it's locked by remote. When he hears this noise he races into the living room and pole-vaults (well, without the pole) into his chair to look out the window, at which point he confirms his suspicion, as he can see the front door of our building, and then he runs to our door to go and wait for Cosmas (aka Daddy). Sometimes I get caught up in the excitement, too, and Cosmas will enter having both dog and wife greeting him with tail-waggings and kisses (Wendell is usually the one who wags his tail and I'm in charge of kisses, but I have been known to wag my tail, too), but on this particular day it was strictly Wendell waiting at the door, alone.

I was actually sitting in our bedroom with the door closed, but I had heard the whole thing play out through the door—Wendell lifting his head with a start and leaping to his feet, Wendell racing to his chair, a pause, and then Wendell racing to the door to wait—and now I could hear the excited hellos being exchanged between a man and his dog. Cosmas, his voice an octave higher than normal, baby-talking Wendell. *Hello. Hello. How's my beautiful boy? How was your day? How was your day? Daddy missed you today. Yes he did. Yes he did.* And I could picture Wendell doing his little twist-and-shout move that he does when really happy, basking in the love, especially today of all days, having been iced out by me all afternoon.

When exactly this big end-of-day lovefest began happening between the two of them, I don't know. Sure, Cosmas was always happy to see Wendell, but it was never quite like this. How funny that I couldn't remember. After a moment I heard Cosmas's tone change a little. "Where's Mommy? Is Mommy home?" And at the mention of the M-word I got mopey once again, as we had just found out that Wendell had no idea who or what the word *Mommy* even referred to.

This was a fairly recent revelation, which we only discovered last week, as a matter of fact, when one night I was in the kitchen cooking dinner, and Cosmas was in the living room trying to watch TV, and Wendell was also in the living room trying to get Cosmas to come down to the floor and wrestle with him instead. After several *nos*, an exasperated Cosmas decided a new tactic was needed and tried an old standby ploy of mine—passing the buck.

I used to hate waking Cosmas up in the mornings, mainly because the process started with "Honeybear, it's time to get up" and then usually ended up thirty minutes later with me shrilling that I was *not* his personal alarm clock, I was *not* his mother, and I was soon *not* going to be his wife if he didn't get his butt out of bed. But now all I had to do was play the "Where's Daddy?" game with Wendell, which involved me saying "Where's Daddy? Where's Daddy? Go get Daddy!" in a very excited voice (the same tone used in saying "Who wants a steak?"), which would result in Wendell making a run for the bedroom and taking a flying leap onto the sleeping Daddy (whereby Wendell would then get an extra treat added to his morning kibble).

But that evening last week when Cosmas said, "Where's Mommy? Where's Mommy? Go get Mommy!" what happened was that Wendell ran out of the living room, zipped right past me in the kitchen, scrambled about in my office, where he found one of his toys under my desk, and went racing back into the living room and thrust it in Cosmas's lap.

Now, I'd be lying if I said this didn't hurt my feelings. (Though let the record show that Cosmas *is* lying when he tells this story and says that I almost started to cry; I was only blinking fast because I had gotten something in my eye.) But, if I did almost cry (which I didn't), could you blame me? I mean, not to sound like an underappreciated martyr, but I do everything for Wendell (feed him, brush him, walk him, take him for car rides, hold his ice-cream cone for him, etc.) and I do it with absolute unconditional love (though perhaps with dogs it's semiconditional, as all the books say you have to make them do tricks for treats), and then to have him think that his Chuck A Duck throw toy was "Mommy," well, it was a little hard to take. (It's not even his favorite toy, for Pete's sake!) I'm not sure if Cosmas had even noticed the transgression when it happened, but he certainly figured it out after the Tater Tots and fish sticks burned in the oven (cooking, warming up—same thing) and then discovered that I had been locked in the bathroom for the last half hour sitting on the floor and sulking over whatever was in my eye.

In the end, Cosmas was finally able to coax me out of the bathroom by explaining that of course Wendell had no idea what *Mommy* really meant, as there was no way he had learned to associate the word with me. He also pointed out that I was absolutely a huge key figure in Wendell's life, much more than even a parental figure—something closer to a god, in a way. (I was always willing to admit to the truth whenever it was presented clearly.)

But tonight, however, it was another matter—even we gods have feelings. So whereas Wendell was probably looking around for some mangy old toy thinking Daddy was ready to play, Cosmas had probably noticed that the bedroom door was closed. Now Cosmas, like most husbands, was aware that a closed bedroom door was never a good sign in general, but the fact that the door was closed and Wendell was on the other side of it was akin to a 5.7 on the Richter scale. So now I heard Cosmas telling Wendell that he'd play with him *later* (a word we wish Wendell understood) and then I heard the sound of his glow ball being tossed across the kitchen (so today Mommy was a glow ball, how swell for me). Then I heard Cosmas walking extremely slowly toward the door, probably praying that it was Wendell who was in the figurative doghouse as opposed to him.

This is when Cosmas opened the door very slowly (no sudden movements). Poking his head in the doorway he said, "Honey, are you okay?" His voice cracked, probably from the stress of realizing that the light wasn't on, which meant that I wasn't even in bed reading magazines—the fact that I was in bed, with the door closed, with the lights off, *and* I was awake and just sitting there, moved the situation from earthquake to Stephen King novel. This was big, and Cosmas was scared.

After seeing that I didn't have a chain saw in my hands, and that both hands were actually visible and not wielding any weapons (well, besides snotty Kleenex balls), he opened the door all the way but still didn't enter.

"Are you okay? Can I come in?"

I nodded, until I saw that Wendell was actually standing directly behind Cosmas and looked like he was about to follow.

"NO!" Cosmas froze. Wendell froze.

"*You* can come in, but not *him*."

Cosmas, still frozen half in and half out, was now trying to figure out whether he was the "you" I was referring to or the "him." I watched as he turned around to see if anyone was behind him, which is when he noticed Wendell.

His posture changed immediately as he now just put it all together and figured out that the closed door, the darkness, and the "him" had nothing to do with him, per se, but with Wendell, and his relief was evident.

"Cosmas, you can come in"—Cosmas was now in the room—"but *your* dog can't." The fact that I had referred to Wendell as his dog stopped him in his tracks again, as never before in the history of Wendell had I ever made reference that Wendell was his dog, in fact I usually referred to Wendell as *my* dog and had to be constantly corrected that he was *our* dog (and I only said this as window dressing because in my secret selfish heart I did feel that Wendell was more mine than his—I mean, who walked him, fed him, brushed him, and took him for car rides? Petty, but true).

Cosmas now turned toward Wendell, who was still on the other side of the doorway, and he shook his head. "Sorry, buddy, but you've got to stay out here." And with that he slowly closed the door on our bewildered dog.

The room was once again dark and Cosmas still had his hand on the door. I leaned to my right and flipped on the lamp.

"You can stop holding your breath, this isn't about you."

Cosmas exhaled noisily. "I'm not holding my breath. So, what's going on?"

"It's not one thing in particular. . . ." I heard Cosmas's breath catch again, as this wasn't what he wanted to hear. He was always better at helping solve an actual concrete problem, as opposed to the ones that were more amorphous.

I continued, "It's just that I don't feel Wendell really appreciates me." Cosmas flinched at this, as this was even worse than he'd thought—it was hard enough when he had to deal with one of my amorphous moods, but if this was now an issue of dealing with the dog's mood, that probably meant the whole Friday night was shot.

Cosmas had a tendency to repeat things when nervous, turning any statement I made into a question and passing it off as a real response. "So, you don't feel that Wendell really appreciates you?"

"That's what I said," I said.

"That's what you said?" he asked back.

"Right," I said.

"Right?" he asked.

I gave him a warning by saying his name in a way an angry bear would say it, if his feelings were hurt and he was about to attack. "Cosmas."

He started to repeat again, "Cos . . ." but caught himself right at the last minute, not wanting to be bear food. "Okay, moving forward. Uhm. So, did something in particular happen today that set you off?"

"Set me off? Why is it automatically assumed that this is all on me?"

"Well, it's just that . . . Uhm. I . . . He's a . . . well . . ."

"Fine, *obviously* he's a dog, so I'm not saying he did what he did with total malicious intent. But *he* knows *better*. I *know* he *knows* better. *Right?*" I challenged, a little unfairly, as there was no way Cosmas was ever going to side against a bear who was stressing every other word.

"Absolutely he should know better, I mean, what could he have been thinking to . . ." He trailed off, now realizing that he actually had no idea what it was that Wendell had done.

"It's not what he did, it's what he didn't do." And then I explained how I had taken Wendell to the park for an hour this afternoon and since there weren't any dogs I played ball with him (this entailed Wendell having the ball and dancing about in front of me rubbing it in my face that I didn't have the ball, and then me saying drop the ball and having him ignore me) and when it was time to go I asked him to come so I could put his lead back on. But not only did he not come to me he also had the audacity to walk over to the mud puddle that he knows he's forbidden to play in and proceeded to walk right into the center of it. So of course I began to scream "No, Wendell!" clapping my hands, which made him jump out of the puddle, and then I asked him to come again, and what did he do? He jumped back in the puddle, so I screamed and charged him, and he got out, and then I stopped midfield and told him to come, and back in the puddle he went. This went on at least three more times and now I was outraged. I mean, have you ever heard of such total insolence? And trust me, there was no way that he didn't know exactly what he was doing.

Now, I like to think that Cosmas said what he said in order to redirect my anger at him as opposed to our dog, who was now whining outside the door, and if this was true, then Wendell certainly owed him one, because it worked, at least for the moment.

"Is that all? I mean, is that all he did?"

Forget the bear; think prehistoric beast. "IS THAT ALL? IS THAT ALL? DID YOU JUST HAVE THE NERVE TO SAY 'IS THAT ALL?' AS FAR AS I'M CONCERNED THAT'S MORE THAN ENOUGH. AND FURTHERMORE . . . [furthermores are never ever good] I CAN'T BELIEVE YOU ARE TAKING HIS SIDE AGAINST ME."

If ever a man regretted saying the words "is that all," it was now. Cosmas immediately hung his head (very similar to the way Wendell did when I finally got him on leash after the mud-puddle experience—ha, further proof that he knew damn well what he did was wrong, or else why would he act so sorry?) and hoped that he could get off the way Wendell normally did, which was by the fact that it was hard to stay annoyed at a dog as cute as Wendell (hence the closed door). No such luck for Cosmas. I pointed to the door, and watched as Cosmas stood up and meekly walked toward it. When he opened it I saw Wendell rush forward with a look of hopefulness, but he soon dropped his ears as Cosmas shook his head—the universal sign of "no go."

In a last attempt of who the hell knows what, Cosmas turned toward me and said, "Remember that time you and I got into a big fight over me saying Wendell was 'just a dog'?"

I grimaced and nodded, as I was pretty sure I knew where he was going with this—yet another mini-lecture about my tendency to get overemotional about the dog, how I took things too seriously when it came to him (he really does ice me out at times if, say, I chintz him on his walks when the weather is nice), and finally to remind me of my three-month-old revelation that perhaps Wendell's wants were actually simple, and that it was I who was the complicated one.

"Well, I know now that he's not just a dog. I guess I didn't understand this before even though you've tried to explain it to me, but I think I understand what you mean now, even though I can't tell you why that is, but even though you don't see him as *just* a dog and now I don't see him as *just* a dog, what we're forgetting is that in doing this we are not remembering to get his opinion on the matter, and I know I can't speak for him, but I wonder whether he might want to point out to us that although he's not *just* a dog, he is, in fact, also a dog. I'm not sure if that's what you want to hear right now, but I thought I'd just toss it out there anyway." The second indicator of Cosmas's unease was to ramble.

All I could do was nod at this, and return his wave after he told me that he was going to take *his* dog out for a walk (pronoun usage duly noted). After a few minutes I heard them both leave, and I was once again alone with my now diminishing anger. Well, one thing was for sure, which was that being angry at your dog was something that was better left in your own head, because as soon as you tried to explain the situation—just saying the words out loud, even—you quickly felt as guilty and foolish as one should feel when annoyed at a dog.

I mean honestly, how could I really be mad at Wendell for playing in the puddle? Even if he was doing it on purpose, it was obvious that he wasn't doing it to spite me (Wendell was so not the spiteful type); it was obvious that he was just being, well, a dog. Who knows, maybe he was doing it thinking that I'd find it amusing, sort of like one of those dumb boy movies where they acted inane just for laughs. And that's when everything became clear, because not knowing was exactly the whole point (okay, I guess I should say things became sort of clear). Wendell was a dog, and as smart as I knew that he was, I still didn't really know what was going on in his mind.

I thought about what Cosmas had said before he left, and how to most it probably didn't make much sense, but that it made plenty of sense to me. Cosmas was not prone to dramatic statements (though he could do a pretty good imitation of Clint's speech in *Unforgiven*), but at least once a year he was able to throw out a zinger that really blew me out of the water, or in this case, out of the bed.

The best part of being irrationally upset was that it was just as easy to irrationally make yourself feel better. I mean, what was the point of moping around in bed on a Friday night, when I could be spending it with my two favorite boys. Quickly grabbing a jacket I threw on my sneakers and headed out the door to go find my husband and my, or rather, *our* dog. I walked down the street and was surprised when I couldn't find them. I continued over to the next street where the park was and as I walked by the public garden I realized that Wendell and Cosmas were in the park on the other side of the fence. But instead of continuing up the street to head into the park, I found myself opening the gate to the garden and sneaking in to see what they were doing. Crouching low under the cover of the overgrown tomato plants and towering sunflowers, I zigzagged through the dark garden until I was close enough to confirm that it was, indeed, Cosmas and Wendell sitting in the dark park.

At first I thought they were just sitting there, but after a moment I realized that Cosmas was talking. I moved in a little closer, hoping Wendell wouldn't hear me and rat me out.

From what I could tell, Cosmas was giving Wendell a little talk. ". . . so like I was saying, I don't really think that Mommy is mad because of the mud factor of the puddle, because remember that time she took you out to play after it rained for a week, I think it was more that she is mad because you were being insensitive to her feelings. So maybe you were joking with the whole jumping in and out of the mud thing, but you've got to learn to figure out when Mommy is in the mood to appreciate a good joke and when she's not. This afternoon, from what I gather, was definitely one of those times when Mommy was not in the mood to appreciate a joke. Does that make sense? And once Mommy gets upset then it's not too hard for the whole thing to snowball, or mudball, or whatever, and next thing you know she's really upset. And trust me, little man, it's not a good thing when Mommy is really upset. Now I know this won't make a lot of sense to you but I'm going to try to explain it to you anyway, okay? It's just that Mommy loves you so much that sometimes when you act badly she feels that you don't appreciate her and this makes her mad, but her being mad is just a cover-up for being sad, remember the whole left-on-the-couch-crink-in-the-neck disaster? Anyway, what you don't understand is that a lot of other mommies are not as nice to their babies, er, doggies, as your mommy is to you.

"So, let's recap. This is a bad puddle. And dogs that play in puddles are bad dogs. And you're a good dog, and good dogs don't play in bad puddles. Bad puddles make Mommy upset. And good dogs like you shouldn't make your mommy upset. That's not good, okay? That's bad. And even though it seems like Mommy gets a bit moody at times, you have to know that she's that way for a reason. No, it's not because she's just moody. Hey, look, it's taken me three years to finally understand her, and I don't want it to take that long for you, because, well, three years is basically twenty-one years in dog years and that's a long time for us all to have to deal with Mommy being upset. I mean, I'll be in my fifties by then . . . no, wait, that's not right, the people-years translation is strictly for dogs, right?"

This is when I turned to go, first because I was about to start laughing, which would blow my cover and would probably embarrass Cosmas, and also because I had heard enough. I couldn't help but smile on my walk home, thinking about Cosmas taking the time to have a heart-to-heart with our dog, the very dog that he wasn't sure that he wanted, and the very dog that got him in trouble, too, just a half hour before. This was the first time that I felt that we were a real family—a family that looked out for each other, a family that loved each other, and a family that was crazy enough to talk to dogs and believe that they understood.

I was in bed reading a magazine with the door open when they came back home twenty minutes later, and it sounded as if Cosmas was now annoyed at Wendell. I heard him take off his collar and command him to sit, as he was going to go and get a towel to wipe off his muddy paws (so much for the no-puddle, bad-puddle pep talk) before Mommy saw him and got mad. At the mention of the word *Mommy*, Wendell was off and running like a shot, and with one big leap, mud flying, he pounced on me, and I squealed with delight. Delight that he disobeyed Daddy in the same way he disobeyed Mommy, but mostly delight that he knew that Mommy loved him, muddy paws and all.

Top Ten Reasons Your Dog Gets More Heavy Petting Than You

1. He has far fewer bad-hair days than you.

2. He is not able to say "I have a headache" (and even if he could, you doubt he'd resort to using such a lame cliché).

3. He is always happy to see you.

4. It's obvious that he would actually do the laundry when he says he would if he could actually do the laundry.

5. He never turns down a belly-rub because he is too full and bloated.

6. He does not work late and does not come home grumpy after working late and immediately want to "relax" in front of the TV.

7. He doesn't only perform for treats—he likes to cuddle.

8. Nine times out of ten he actually does what he is told.

9. He looks at you with total and complete adoration even when you have a big zit.

10. He knows how to shake his tail to get what he wants.

The 10 Breeds of Obsessed Dog Owners

7. The Oblivious Owner

This is the dog owner who is very passive and really doesn't pay that much attention to his dog. His dog is normally the bully and is continually chasing down other dogs and flipping them as if they are tiddly-winks. His dog tends to hump every dog in sight no matter if the other dog is crying and whimpering and clawing the ground to get away. This dog owner just shrugs when you are hysterically trying to get your dog away from his dog and says things like "Oh, they're just playing." "I'm sure that's just a little scratch." "Yes, that looks like blood, but I'm sure your dog is fine." "Hmmm, you're right, it does appear that he is holding an ear in his mouth, well I'll be darned." And of course his motto, his mantra, is "Dogs will be dogs."

8

Have You Updated Your Will with Provisions for Your Dog?

SHOULD HE STAY OR SHOULD HE GO?

It was that time of year; twenty thousand gastroenterologists all over the world were starting to lick their lips in anticipation of the biggest medical event in their business—Digestive Disease Week. A five-day extravaganza of everything intestinal—doctors, researchers, drug companies all gathering in San Francisco to meet, eat, and shop (okay, maybe not everyone would be shopping, but you could bet your sweet bottom that's what the spouses would be doing—I mean, why else attend a boring medical convention?). It happened to be my husband's first time going, and when we'd booked the trip almost six months before, I was giddy with excitement—finally getting to partake in the perks of being a doctor's wife: free hotel (really close to Neiman's), free food (as long as we ate cheap and made it look like it was a meal for one), and approximately six thousand frequent-flier miles (our generation's own Green Stamps).

But one Sunday morning a month or so before we were supposed to leave, I woke up from a horrible nightmare with the sudden knowledge that I couldn't go—not because I didn't *want* to go (and shop), but because I simply couldn't leave Wendell behind.

Knowing Cosmas would flip out at the news, I pretended to still be asleep until he'd risen and walked off to take his shower. Cosmas was always happy in the shower, but Sundays were the pinnacle, as I generally allowed him to stay in as long as he desired (the hell with everyone else in the building getting any hot water). Also, I figured it was a good time to make my announcement, since he wouldn't be able to make a big to-do about it, being at a slight disadvantage (i.e., naked, wet, and holding a purple body sponge shaped like a hippo wearing a tutu).

So after waiting a few minutes I got up and walked into the bathroom and began to tell Cosmas about my nightmare—the big thugs in trench coats, the blood on the floor, and a small furry body being rolled up in a Persian-rug floor runner. After running on for a while without so much as an "Uh-huh, that's nice" from Cosmas, I made my move, casually slipping in the part about my nightmare being some kind of an omen and the fact that I'd decided it was best that I not go on our trip after all. I held my breath for his outburst . . . but it didn't come. Well, okay—great, then!

I was just sighing with relief and turning to leave when

Cosmas ripped open the shower curtain, his head a sham-
pooed meringue, and barked, "What?! What did you say?"
(Guess the water in his ears must have caused a delayed reaction. . . .)

I tried to bolt, but he was too fast and grabbed my wrist.
For a brief moment I considered whether I'd be able to chew
my arm off to get away. Thinking better of it, I began to go
through the motions of crying (lowering my gaze, sniffling,
blinking rapidly in hope of dislodging a contact and produc-
ing actual tears). Just then, my peripheral vision caught a
furry figure darting past the doorway. Wendell on a recon-
naissance mission to see why the water was running (and
dreading the possibility that it might be intended for *him*).

This only strengthened my maternal resolve and, ready
now to express my very sound and logical reasoning, I took a
deep breath and prepared to make the case. When I opened
my mouth to take Cosmas calmly through my thinking,
however, what actually came out was my most *insanely* annoying whine, as I began to rant: "What if our *plane* goes down?
What will happen to Wendell? We haven't even changed our
will yet. In fact, we don't even have a will! So then what?
We're dead and Wendell is going to go from foster home to
foster home where he's mistreated and abused. Do you think
any foster parent is actually going to take the time to brush
him every day? You know the way he mats. He'll be a Rastafarian with dreadlocks in no time. Remember what happened in *White Oleander*, how that poor little girl chopped off
all her gorgeous blond hair and eventually dyed it black—I

mean, she went totally Goth! Is that what you want to happen? And when he finally manages to escape from the foster parents, then what? A life doing tricks on the street?" By the time I paused for breath, I burst right into tears. But for real, this time.

Cosmas had been standing with one leg out of the shower and one leg in, and by now his soft-serve shampoo head had melted all down his body to form a milky white puddle on the floor below. His eyes were now bloodshot from the suds, and it was unclear whether his rapid blinking was from stinging pain or the desperate hope that I was just some raving hologram, like Princess Leia from *Star Wars*, and might just disappear in a second. Then, without saying a word, he simply stepped back into the shower and pulled the curtain closed on me.

It was then that Wendell appeared in the doorway, though he was standing a good six inches away, suspicious that all the commotion was just an elaborate ruse on our part to get him into a bath. I saw the tension in his legs, as he was poised and ready to run like hell if I even breathed in his direction. He sniffed the air a bit, and then eyed the shampoo puddle on the floor by the tub. He licked his nose.

"No, it is *not* ice cream," I said, quickly grabbing some toilet paper to sop it up before he had time to decide whether melty ice cream might actually be worth the risk of entering the bathroom even when the water was running.

After cleaning up the mess, I sat down on the tiles and threw out my arms, signaling Wendell that I needed some

TLC. Normally he'd come running, as he loved to sit in my lap while I baby-talked him and smothered him with kisses (or at least he loved the beef-flavored rawhide I generally gave him during such endearments). But this time, picking up on my stress, Wendell took my arm motion to mean B-A-T-H (we have to spell it out), and shot me a look of betrayal—*How dare you try to lure me with hugs, kisses, and ice cream? Did I have no shame?*—and took off toward the living room.

Time flies when you're plunged into the lethargy of complete indecision, and ten minutes later, I was still slumped down on the floor, staring at my shredded cuticles. Cosmas had to be pretty desperate to get out of the shower by now. Finally he turned off the water, but instead of pulling back the shower curtain, his arm reached out uncertainly, feeling around for each of the three towels that were hanging on the rack to find the one that was the *most* dry (Cosmas has some thing about damp towels, and always insists on a towel that is very, very dry). Then, pulling in the third towel he came to, he started to dry himself off behind the curtain.

I knew I should've just given the guy a break and headed into another room so he could try to salvage a tiny sliver of happiness from his whole Sunday bathroom experience, but I didn't. Another minute passed, and then from behind the shower curtain I heard a sigh, followed by a quiet voice. "Why don't we just bring him?"

Now, it's not that I hadn't thought about bringing Wendell along, because when we booked the trip he was half his current size, and I just assumed that he'd come along, too.

I had even reserved a convertible for our trip, as we were heading to Carmel for two days after the conference ended. Yes, the three of us zipping down Route 1 in our shiny red Ford Mustang rental car—the California sun picking up the little flecks of red in his hair, the breeze whipping through his mat-free gorgeous mane. *If I put a little lemon in his hair, perhaps he'd get even blonder; when in Rome, right?* But Wendell was now well over the limit for bringing him on board, having reached the exact average adult weight for his breed (forty pounds). Which meant that he'd have to be crated up and put in cargo. Which . . . how should I put this?—wasn't going to happen.

Cosmas coughed. Oh, right; I hadn't answered him. Now it was my turn to sigh. "No, we can't bring him. The flight's too long, and can you imagine how loud it would be in cargo, and you know he's sensitive to noise. . . . Remember that story I heard about where all the cargo shifted in flight and the dog's crate got all wedged in and the poor dog almost asphyxiated . . . can you imagine? Poor Wendell sitting in the dark, fighting for every breath . . ."

At this, Cosmas whipped open the shower curtain and began to stab his raisin-wrinkly finger at me. "*You are going* to DDW. *We* are going to DDW. This is crazy." Then as he stepped out onto the bath mat, he lowered his voice and tried Good Cop. "C'mon honey, we've been planning this trip for months . . . and I know you've already downloaded the layout of Union Square's shopping district into your Sony Clie. Think about it. Neiman Marcus. Saks Fifth Avenue. Burberry. Prada. Chanel. Barneys . . ."

"Hellllooooo, there *is* no Barneys in San Fran. Only L.A."

He pulled me up off the floor and gave me a big hug and started trying to dance me around the bathroom, singing, "La la la, Diesel jeans . . . la la la . . . Gucci . . . la la la . . . Calvin Klein . . . la la Dolce and the Cabana Boy!" I laughed at this, and as I relaxed into him, started to waver a bit. He was right, I mean, I *had* only been to San Fran two times before, and both had been business trips where I hadn't had the opportunity to shop at all. Plus, I'd never been to Carmel before, *and* we'd be staying at a really, *really* nice hotel. . . .

Now that the water was off, Wendell appeared in the bathroom doorway again. He watched us dance about the bathroom and then did that cute thing where he jumps up, wanting to be a part of the family hug. We let him join in, and soon we were all in bed, Wendell on a towel happily chewing on a rawhide, and Cosmas and I stretched out making up a master pros-and-cons list of whether or not he should stay or go. Cosmas wrote down the main "pro-stay" argument, which was the fact that Wendell *did* love to play with other dogs and would probably have a blast at any dog hotel we booked him into. I countered that pro with the con and wrote, "What if he plays himself to death?!" with a little frowny face for emphasis. Cosmas sighed and used his one veto vote to scratch it off the list, telling me that from a medical standpoint, such a thing was virtually impossible.

And so began our search for Wendell's home away from home, as there was no way I'd ever put him in the kind of dog kennel consisting of a doghouse outside on a slab of concrete surrounded by a chain-link fence. (Outside. Can you believe it—outside?! I shudder at the very thought of what the elements could do to a dog's coat.) I had heard that well-brought-up dogs could stay at places called hotels (or "bed-and-biscuits"), where, instead of being caged up, the dogs are allowed to play together, eat together, and sleep together. The best places could boast of antiques, comfy sofas, and full coil spring beds where the dogs could freely lounge about and watch the free HBO that was a part of the package.

Going strictly by who took out the biggest ads in the phone book (after all, nothing wrong with showing off in certain areas), which ones were the most expensive (hey, you get what you pay for), and which ones had received the "Best of Boston" award the most times, I narrowed the search down to the one place that I thought seemed okay. On calling, I was told that before they'd accept a dog for day care and overnight stays, the dog would have to be interviewed, and I was told very clearly that there were "no guarantees" about acceptance.

Of course, I liked the fact that the place demanded in-person visits and was discriminating enough not to let in any old riffraff. But on further consideration, I couldn't help but be slightly put off by the fact that *they* held all the power in the situation. Weren't *we* the clients? Weren't *we* supposed to be the ones doing the interviewing? What about the list of twenty-seven questions that I had prepared? The very thought that Wendell might not make the cut caused my already hyperneurotic tendencies to kick into overdrive, and I found myself unable to sleep the night before the interview.

I had been lying in the dark for the past three hours, and was now at the point where I was obsessing about what *I* was going to wear to the interview. Wendell was dead asleep at my feet, having been bathed, trimmed, and combed within an inch of his life earlier in the day. His favorite dog collar (or rather, *our* favorite dog collar) was now drying on a towel in the bathroom after having been scrubbed clean with a tooth-brush, his dog tags had been buffed until they gleamed, and I even had a few leaves in a Ziploc bag that I planned to place in his hair right before we went in (to show that he wasn't a little froufrou prima donna and knew how to have a good time).

Cosmas, too, was asleep—or at least pretending to be, probably so he wouldn't have to discuss the interview any-more. It had already been decided that Cosmas would be coming with us to the interview, as I felt that it was important to show them Wendell came from a strong family unit. Cosmas had balked at my suggestion that he wear a white doctor's jacket or at the very least manage to have his stetho-scope jauntily slung about his neck, but had finally given in to agreeing to "play doctor" when my friend Anne paged him in the middle of the interview. I told him to keep the "fake" call quick (so as not show that he took his work more seriously than our family life) but to properly convey his affiliation with Mass General Hospital, as you never know who knew someone who was on the liver-donor list (of course, Cosmas had no real discretion about such things, but as I explained to him over and over, "perception is reality in the new millennium").

That was just how these things worked, quid pro quo—they had the power to not let Wendell into their bed-and-biscuit, and *we* had the power to make their colonoscopy a really unpleasant experience. Besides, getting Wendell in would only be the first step, because even more important was to have him placed on their internal VIP (very important pooch) list. You'd be crazy not to think that some dogs didn't get a little extra-special treatment in such places. For a moment, I found myself regretting that I was married only to a doctor and not some temperamental mobster who could really "break it down" for everyone.

I'd already decided that I wasn't going to wear a suit to the interview, but didn't want to be seen as a total stay-at-home dog-mom either—one of those owners who has too much time on her hands and would be flagged as a high-maintenance pain in the ass, always calling to check in on her dog at odd hours, and just isn't worth the hassle (let them find this out later, when it's too late!). I was pretty sure that I was going to wear my Paper Denim & Cloth jeans (which would suggest how down-to-earth I was and how unafraid I'd be of getting on the floor for some serious playtime), a white pressed button-down shirt, untucked (you know—I'd be easygoing enough to wear white in the presence of dogs, and anything but uptight or overly fastidious), and my sky blue quilted Burberry vest (which would convey a fun fashion flair, but with a sporty, out-doorsy, likes-to-take-walks-in-the-woods-but-would-always-check-for-ticks-right-afterward level of seriousness).

I watched the clock blink 3:37 A.M. and decided that I needed to get some sleep. I mean, if I appeared with dark circles under my eyes, wouldn't they kind of infer that Wendell was a rowdy night owl who would disturb the other dogs' bedtime?

Due to the fact that the trailer-tractor highway accident I'd been factoring in never actually happened, we arrived at the Bed & Biscuit an hour early. I didn't want to appear overeager, so we parked at a nearby doughnut shop, and I left the boys in the car munching on doughnuts (Cosmas with a chocolate glazed and Wendell with a strawberry jelly) as I went to scope the outer perimeter of the facilities. The fence was in good shape as far as I could tell, and there didn't seem to be any industrial dumping grounds nearby. Pulling an Erin Brockovich, I pretended to tie my boots while nonchalantly checking out the dogs playing in the yard—all of whom appeared to be friendly and well groomed.

Finally, at ten minutes till our appointed time, I artfully placed two broken leaf pieces in Wendell's hair, and we entered the building. I took a deep breath through my nose and exhaled in relief—no rank smell—so far so good.

We were escorted into a small office with a table and the manager sat down with us. I handed her the file folder already color-coded with Wendell's name and license number. She smiled as she flipped through the folder containing his entire health record as well as a few premade "lost" signs in case he managed to escape on their watch (for the authorities and local news). Her smile seemed to indicate that she was impressed with my record-keeping, and not simply humoring a possible asylum escapee.

She went over the rules and regulations and handed us a few forms to sign. I eyeballed them quickly and was just about to ask whether we could fax them in later (after I showed them to our lawyer, of course), but Cosmas whipped out the MGH hospital pen that I had planted in his front pocket (turned out Anne had to attend a last-minute meeting) and signed them without so much as a cursory glance. I bit my tongue and looked around the room at the framed "award" certificates that were hanging on the wall. I also noticed a white T-shirt with red lettering that said "My Dog Went to the Bed & Biscuit and All He Got Me Was a Lousy T-shirt" displayed for sale. Granted, the joke was a bit lame, but suddenly I wanted it—badly. I reveled in the thought of myself at the local dog park wearing it with the blue vest I now had on (red and baby blue—ohmygod: darling).

Cosmas's hand on my shoulder woke me up from my fashion reverie, and I noticed that everyone was now standing; apparently it was time for Wendell's interview. As we walked over to the main playroom, the manager explained their core philosophy regarding the need for a true "pack hierarchy." She told us that the *owner's* dog was the alpha male (makes sense, right?), and that every dog had to show due respect for his position of authority. She was now going to have the dogs meet each other one-on-one, and if all went well she would let in a few other dogs to see how they all interacted as a group.

She took Wendell's leash from me and, as I started to follow her into the room, stopped me. It would be best, she said, if we weren't present to distract him, but we were welcome to watch over the gate. I gritted my teeth and smiled, grabbing Cosmas's hand for reassurance. Wendell was now running around the room by himself, smelling all along the walls. I squeezed Cosmas's hand even harder as it dawned on me that Wendell might try to pee on the wall to mark it as his own. But just then the manager came back in with a large German shepherd named Howard.

Wendell ran over to Howard, and as they began to smell each other I braced myself for Wendell's normal M.O., which is to try to invoke play by pouncing on the other dog's shoulder. But while Wendell's tail was certainly going a mile a minute, somehow he managed to stand totally still while Howard completed two full circles around him. I saw the manager nod in their direction, and then the door opened a second time. Two more dogs entered this time—a Labrador and a French bulldog.

Wiping my watering eyes, I realized I'd been holding my breath too long. Quietly and with as much control as possible, I tried to exhale as we watched Wendell and Mandy, the Labrador, begin to frolic and play. I studied the manager studying them . . . and was pleased to note that *she* seemed pleased. *All right,* I said to myself, loosening up a bit, *maybe everything's gonna work out just fine here. . . .*

This is when Wendell broke away, ran to the far-right corner, and proceeded to hunch over into the "number-two" position.

Aghast, and completely oblivious to the gate in my path, I charged forward, clapping my hands loudly, hoping to distract him from the operation at hand (or would that be "hind"?). Every dog in the room froze and stared at me. Except for Wendell. Who simply finished his excretions, paused a moment to collect himself, and then quickly rejoined the group. I felt the color drain from my face, certain in the knowledge that I wouldn't be wearing my new T-shirt to bed that night after all. . . .

Horrified, I looked over at Cosmas, but all he could give me was a helpless shrug of surprise. I was just about to charge into the room to grab Wendell and run away in shame when the manager appeared in front of the gate. Shaking her head, she leaned in to say something, and I lowered my eyes to the ground, unable even to look her in the eye. It took me a moment or two to register as she assured me that Wendell's "accident" was totally normal and that many other dogs had done the same before him, which he clearly must have known by smell, figuring it was okay to follow suit. I nodded, my frown of seriousness dispersing with pride. Wendell always *had* been extremely perceptive.

Next thing I knew, everyone was shaking hands and the

three of us (plus two new T-shirts) were walking out the door. Cosmas and I high-fived as soon as we got into the car, and we all celebrated with another trip to the doughnut shop. Later that night, wearing my new T-shirt, I called all five of the references the Bed & Biscuit had given us, grilling each dog owner thoroughly (and using trick questions just to make sure these "references" weren't related to any of the B&B employees), and as I got off the phone with the last person I knew that we had indeed found the perfect place.

We even took their suggestion and scheduled an overnight stay for Wendell just to show him that "we'd be back for him." He returned to us only slightly smelly, and with no discernible symptoms of post-traumatic stress disorder. I, on the other hand, had gone berserk from missing him, threatening to drive there in the middle of the night so I could scale the wall and spring him (Cosmas had refused to join me in this mission of love and force-fed me a few Tylenol PMs instead).

In the end it was decided that I would indeed be joining Cosmas for his trip to California. I drew out an extensive to-do list of everything that had to be taken care of before we left: Cosmas would get a will drawn up with provisions and strict guidelines for Wendell-care; I would put together a questionnaire that I could give to our top three potential "dog-godparent" couples who might be suitable to take care of Wendell should something happen to us (there was a time when I was just going to let my brother John and his wife, Susie, take Wendell if the need ever arose, but once when casually quizzing my brother about whether he would give Wendell mouth-to-mouth in an emergency situation he started to laugh and thought I was joking, so now he's going to have to prove he's the best guardian the same as everyone else); Cosmas was going to research whether it made sense for us to travel separately, so at least one of us would be around if a plane happened to go down; and lastly, I was going to research the dog foster-care system on the off chance that, the very day we died, the highest-scoring dog-godparents (as well as their runners-up) might somehow have died as well.

When we were finished, Cosmas and I both initialed our specific task entries and signed at the bottom of the page. Afterward I felt much better, and soon I was tucked back into bed studying my map of the San Francisco shopping district (figuring that it would be better if I just memorized all the store locations so I wouldn't have to keep pulling out my map).

And, by the way, what kind of pups and young dogs' department would Neiman's have anyway? . . .

The Top Ten Breeds of People Who (Obviously) Don't Have a Dog

1. The I used to have a dog like fifty years ago and even though I haven't had one in half a century and I don't know you or your dog I'm still going to tell you what I think about your dog and compare him to my dead dog, who was the best dog in the entire world [and who also happens to sound an awful lot like Old Yeller, having saved his life from a pack of wild boars and then having to be shot after acquiring rabies—hello, that *is* Old Yeller!].

2. The ohmygod your dog is so cute and I love dogs and I have a dog but he stays with my parents, which really breaks my heart but I'm just too busy with work and dating to take care of my dog but I really miss him and do you think it would be okay if I pet your dog even though it's obvious you are in a rush and are carrying groceries and your dry cleaning, but I promise I'll only play with him for like ten minutes or so, would that be okay?

3. The excuse me but can I give your dog a cookie that I just happen to have in my pocket even though I don't have a dog with me and might not even have a dog but I'm weird

enough to just carry around dog biscuits in one of my four-teen pockets in my army fatigues and would you like to see an old knife-wound scar I have on my arm?

4. The look how good that dog is behaving here in the very cramped quarters of the ATM vestibule on a very busy Friday night and I just can't believe how nicely that dog is just sitting there next to his owner, so calm and sweet and I wonder what such a calm and well-behaved dog would do if I started to make faces at him, like sticking my tongue out at him like I haven't done since the third grade which was fine since I was like seven then and it was socially acceptable behavior back then and even though it's not anymore since I'm like forty I think it would be fun to make faces at the dog and hey, I know what would be even funnier, maybe I'll bark at your dog, wouldn't that be funny if I barked at the very calm and well-behaved dog. *Bark bark bark.* Wait a second, do you know what would be even funnier? Maybe I should meow at the dog like I'm a cat. *Meow. Meow. Meow.* Oh look, the calm dog is now getting all antsy and is lunging at me and barking back and now its poor owner is embarrassed and has to leave the ATM line when she was so close to getting to the head of the line.

5. The I'm a cat person who really feels that cats are quite superior to dogs in every way and I can prove that this is true and of course I can write an essay on the subject because

I'm not going out on Saturday night this weekend because I'm going to stay at home and clean out my cat's kitty litter.

6. The I'm really really scared of dogs so much that I will either cross the street when I see your dog is coming or will instead go out of my way to walk a very wide arc around your dog just in case it manages to break away from your grip and lunge for me ready to tear out my throat. And don't think I'm an alarmist because I've heard that even small dogs can be killers.

7. The relative (i.e., mother) who feels that you are spending way too much money, time, and attention on your dog when you should be spending more of your money, time, and attention on her or your husband, hence the lack of grandchildren. This relative (i.e., Mom) says things like "Don't even tell me you are getting a birthday cake or more toys for your dog" whenever you tell her that it is your dog's birthday.

8. The hey you don't know me but I would like to get to know your dog if you don't mind though I'm not going to ask and in fact I'm going to stride right up to your dog and just start petting him on the head and speaking baby talk to your dog and asking what his name is and how long you've had him and then when he's jumping up on me because I'm patting my thighs and saying here boy, here big guy, I will

pet him some more even as you are pulling your dog off me and explaining that your dog is not allowed to jump up on people and then I'll tell you that I don't mind and in fact I like when dogs jump on me and I think it's cute and who cares if you've been specifically training him not to do it and why don't you just lighten up a little because after all he is a dog and he just wants to show his love for people.

9. The cranky homeowner who has built up an almost comic-book hatred of all dogs due to the fact that they pee in his yard and kill his shrubs and he spends all his time looking out the second-floor window of his house just waiting for some poor unsuspecting dog to come walking along so that he can run down the stairs and burst through the front door, scaring both the dog and the owner, and start swearing at the dog and screaming about the boundaries of public versus private property and then go on to explain how many times he's had to re-place his front shrub all because of stupid dogs. As the mean person catches his breath from screaming and wipes the spittle off his face, you should then explain in a very calm and polite voice that although you appreciated all that he had to say, you seriously doubt that your dog un-derstood him, mainly because your dog doesn't speak asshole!

10. The good friend or colleague who is convinced that your attachment to your dog is borderline obsessive (though behind your back she says you're a total obsessive) and rolls her eyes every time you bring up your dog and the cute things that your dog does and is never interested in looking at your latest pictures that you've taken of your dog. This is the friend who totally makes fun of you when she talks to her other friends, so much so that all her friends only know of you as the crazy dog lady, and when you meet these friends you can tell that they are having problems remembering your real name and they can't help but throw in a little snarky comment like "Oh, right, I've heard so much about you *and your dog*." (The proper response to this comment is to say, "Really, that's funny, I've never heard her say anything about you at all.")

The 10 Breeds of Obsessed Dog Owners

8. The Owner Whose *Human* Family Comes Second...

At first glance these dog owners seem to be like any other obsessed dog owner—believing that their dogs happen to be the most special dogs in the world, and even though they love all dogs they secretly like their dogs best. But where they differ enough to get their own category is that their love for their dogs is so great that everything and *everyone* else pales in comparison. The human children of these dog owners make wry jokes to their friends about the fact that their parents loved their dog more than they loved them, but then no one really laughs. Naturally their friends say, "Of course your parents didn't love their dog more than they loved you, that's crazy talk." So then the victimized child says, "Oh yeah? I'll prove it to you," and she takes her friends to her parents' home so they can see that for every *one* picture of her displayed, there are, like, *five* pictures of the dog (in nicer frames), and then she points out that the dog's diplomas are in the living room and that her own diploma is hanging in the bathroom (again, in a cheaper frame). Her friends now feel bad and she feels worse, but is thankful that dogs don't live forever or there would be no money left in the will for the actual bipedal offspring.

Are You Plagued by Irrational Fears of Your Dog's Untimely Demise?

ON FROZEN POND

I was six years old when we went for an atypical Saturday-morning family drive. I remember waving good-bye to Julie, our dog, who was uncharacteristically tied up front-and-center in our driveway. When we returned an hour later Julie was gone. I was told that she ran away to join the circus, but I later found out that she had bitten the gas meter reader and, well, probably did not become a circus dog. (Of course, I like to think that she managed to escape her horrible fate and was taken in by the fat lady and the sad clown, who treated her really well.) Two years later, Jet, our two-year-old beagle, just disappeared. Four years later, Scottie, our cocker spaniel, was found dead at the tender age of two. (I was told it was something she ate, but ascertained through hushed tones and closed doors that a foul-play poisoning was suspected.)

Oscar, my favorite, was a black Labrador I had when I was

fourteen. Oscar was sweet, lovable, and known for trying a little too hard to please (when I taught him to fetch the paper, he fetched not only ours, but everyone else's in the neighborhood). He was hit by a car while chasing Spike, another neighborhood dog, who had a penchant for chasing cars. He lingered for four days after my father, an orthopedic surgeon, helped our local vet reconstruct his poor broken skull, but he didn't make it.

Dexter, our second black Lab, was a quick fix of a young girl's broken heart, but he proved to be as wild as Oscar had been sweet. After thousands of dollars in obedience schools, Dexter tipped over the meanest man in the neighborhood's trash one too many times and was sent to the farm. (Don't worry; it was an actual farm, as opposed to a "farm in the sky.")

Bringing up the rear was Sacha, a German shepherd mix I bought on the street for twenty bucks when I was sixteen. If I had known how to find Julie I would have contacted the circus and let them know we had found an escape artist who left Houdini in the dust. Three different fences later, Sacha joined Dexter on a local farm.

So, of course you can imagine that I was now totally paranoid about Wendell's untimely demise. In fact, I became a projectionary hypochondriac, thinking that every nuance of Wendell's mood implied imminent death. A hawk could take lessons from me as I watched his every move. As a young pup he was plagued with colitis (which is actually amusing since Cosmas is a gastroenterologist, though he doesn't find it quite as amusing as I do). I dutifully kept a puppy poo-poo journal, noting every single bowel movement he had in terms of time, size, color, and consistency. I read about worms that are only found in the flatlands of Africa and called my vet asking him to screen Wendell. (No. He has never been to Africa. No, I have never been to Africa. But perhaps he came in contact with some other dog whose owner had just come back from Africa. This is Cambridge, so I'm sure there are some Harvard African-grassland studies going on, don't you think?)

One fear I had was that perhaps Wendell had some sort of hormone gland problem, as I was certain that his tongue was growing faster than it should. It's just that a lot of times when Wendell was napping (though he never got to nap for too long, as I was constantly pulling a Shirley MacLaine from *Terms of Endearment* and waking him up to make sure he didn't have sudden puppy death syndrome), about a centimeter of his tongue would be protruding from his mouth. Surely such a thing was not normal. Wouldn't his tongue dry out by being exposed to the air that way? What if it deadened his taste buds? Even though I couldn't find anything about a rare tongue-growth disorder on the Internet (even when typing in that long-tongued guy from Kiss), I was sure that something was wrong. Sometimes when Wendell woke up his tongue appeared to be so dried out that it was sort of stuck to his top lip, ew. After two days of being reassured by my husband (who is *not* an Ear Nose Throat doctor), our vet, and about five more vets in the area (I was calling around disguising my voice, saying I was a visiting research student from Africa, just in case they might warn me of African grassland worm disease for dogs), I took matters into my own hands. I bought an eyedropper and stood watch, and gently dropped water onto his tongue to make sure it stayed fresh and moist.

I will say the worst scenarios of Wendell's macabre death played out in my head. How he managed to figure out how to work the dead-bolt lock and went running out into the street to be hit by a speeding cab. How some crazed doggie hit men would break into the house and rough him up, looking for information (a case of mistaken identity). How some rogue scientists would kidnap him to perform horrible experiments, hooking him up to electrodes and making him push levers for a pellet of dry, tasteless dogfood. I will say that in my mind, whenever such visions plagued me, I was always able to regain control of the fantasy and swoop in to save my beloved darling dog. How I'd wake up in the middle of the night, hearing the downstairs door slam shut. How I'd race downstairs and into the street, shielding his furry frame from the oncoming cab (so I'd break a few ribs, big deal). How I'd scare away the thugs by doing my own version of the Karate Kid stance, and how they'd run away, having just seen *Crouching Tiger, Hidden Dragon* and thinking that perhaps I was a distant cousin of Bruce Lee (because all Asians are related in some way or another, right?). And lastly, how I'd track down those rogue scientists, breaking into their high-tech security labs (with my low-tech bobby pin) and freeing Wendell as well as all the other animals they had captured (front page of *USA Today*, baby!).

As much as I thought I was prepared for every emergency (the numbers of poison control taped to the fridge and pull-outs of dog CPR taped to the wall), I found that you can never really be prepared for an emergency when it arises, or in my case, when it cracks wide open.

The only comparison I can make of what the Fresh Pond Reservoir found in Cambridge, Massachusetts, is like for dogs is that it's probably similar to what Disneyland is for small children. Meaning that as a parent, it's something you must suffer through, but that it certainly makes a dent in your sanity. This park is one of the few places in the Boston area where dogs are legally allowed off leash (provided that your dog follows oral commands—which Wendell does, but only when we're at home and I'm holding a treat, but hey, rules-schmules) and given the chance to run wild in the open fields, traipse through the wooded areas, and splash about in a small pond at the edge of a neighboring golf course, which is on the far side of the two-mile loop around the reservoir.

When we first got Wendell and I was trying to prove that I was the nicest doggy parent around I would try to take him there at least once a weekend. But the frequency started to diminish a bit as Wendell was a little hard to control there. Now, granted, I loved his upbeat personality and his natural doggy curiosity in everyday life, but when unleashed at Fresh Pond he became an entirely different beast (and don't think I'm using the word *beast* lightly) altogether; basically, he was like a dog on crack. His normal M.O. was to first tear around like a missile without a target—looping wide circles and then zigzagging all about from every tree to dog to owner to dog to stick to mud puddle to anything that would stick to his fur (which was a lot), all the while he would be suddenly struck totally deaf and would not even give me a glance, no matter how I bellowed his name. It was this bellowing that was another reason why it wasn't high on my list of places to visit.

I can't speak for other dog owners, but what I can say is that there have been times when I've romanticized about my own image as a dog owner. In my head I've always seen myself as that tall, thin, elegant (helloo! This a fantasy so I'm allowed a little artistic license, I think), well-dressed but somewhat mysterious dog owner who looks quite dramatic and soulful in all outdoorsy settings—very black-and-white Ansel Adams photo-ish but with me wearing some kick-ass coat with a hood. But of course in all actuality I know that I'm about as far from this image as you can get, meaning that most days when I'm out schluffing around my neighborhood with Wendell I'm usually in jeans, sneakers (though I do wear too-cool-for-school Pumas), some random jacket, and it would be considered a good day if I actually had clean hair and was wearing lipstick.

And at Fresh Pond I seem to become larger than life as well, but not in a good way, as I normally have some crazed expression on my face, my eyes darting back and forth as I'm trying to keep track of my zigzagging dog. I'm usually red in the face from trying to run after him, and I'm loud. Yes, there, I said it. I am that loud owner who is running about in the park screaming after her dog that all the other dog owners can't help but notice and snicker over, clicking their little judgmental tongues about how it's owners like me that mar the image of dog owners everywhere. (Sigh.) Basically, it's not the best look for either of us.

So on this particular day at Fresh Pond I was with my good friend, neighbor, and fellow dog-mommy Carrie (mother to Wendell's best friend, Thatcher, a golden retriever, named after Margaret Thatcher), and we were trying to get a little exercise in ourselves by walking the loop. I will say that Wendell is usually a little more in control when in the company of Carrie and Thatcher, as I believe he understands that we are invoking the laws of pack animals and that he should at least try to stay within fifty feet of us. (Of course the only way I can even get him out of the main field and onto the path is that I have to wave my arms like a lunatic and run screaming down the path, at which point Wendell may or may not decide to follow.)

So there we were on our nature walk, the dogs happily running ahead, and Carrie and I walking behind them and catching up on each other's day-to-day lives—discussing current events, books we've read, art exhibits we'd like to see. This goes on for about fifteen minutes until we run out of deep things to philosophize about and then move on to more serious matters at hand—celebrities. Who was foolish enough to feel she was actually pretty enough to pull off bangs. Who was chunking out. Who was getting skinny, and what drugs we assumed she was on to be so thin. Who was dating whom. Who wore what god-awful thing to the award-show-of-the-moment. Who was dumping whom. Who obviously had work done, etc. And of course what we'd be doing if we were fabulously rich, thin, on drugs, and had figures that made even sweatsuits look good.

By now we were at the far side of the loop and it just so happened that the golf-course pond was still partially frozen over even though we were a few weeks into spring (damn those never-ending New England winters!), and when I looked up to see what mud puddle Wendell was rolling in at the moment I found him twenty feet out, standing on the frozen ice in the middle of the pond. He was just standing there, finally calm and serene, looking almost regal and out of this world as if walking on water were an everyday event. I gasped and nudged Carrie.

I almost didn't want to say anything, afraid that mere words would break the spell of this wonderful picture-perfect moment, but of course I did say something, and of course it was loud. "Holy *&#^*&! Why is it that I never have a camera when I need one? I mean, look how great he looks right now. I mean, wouldn't this be just the perfect Christmas-card picture? If you capture it the right way, it would almost look like he's walking on water. Hmmm, is that blasphemous? God, all I need is the Catholic Church on my case. . . ."

Totally lost in my ramblings, it probably took Carrie at least a few elbows in the arm for me to finally shut my mouth.

Carrie, also transfixed by the scene before us, but always the more proper one, the more level-headed one, and the one least likely to be loud and overdramatic, said, "Jenny, I wonder if it's really that safe for him to be out there. . . . I mean, what if the ice starts to break?"

Scenes from *Little House on the Prairie* flashed before my eyes, predominantly the "Blizzard" episode in Season 3 when the sweet blond schoolteacher let the kids go home early when it started snowing and then whammo, those five little flakes turned into a raging blizzard of epic proportions and pretty soon the whole town was freaking out and all the parents were yelling at the teacher, who was sobbing because the fates of all the little children on the prairie were in her hands (well, except for Nellie and Willie, who had to stay behind after school to clean the erasers and it's not like they could carry the show on their own anyway), as they were all now lost in the snow since they all had to walk, like, seven miles to and from school each day. I thought about Charles's grim expression as he tried to comfort Caroline (honestly, how many tragedies can one woman take?), I thought about the preacher trying to offer the deranged parents some comfort, all the while looking pretty skeptical, and I racked my brain to remember who exactly perished in the storm (someone always perishes). Which then led me to remember that there actually wasn't a scene in this particular episode where kids were falling through the ice, and given this fact I wasn't sure what the appropriate response would be if such a thing were to occur.

It was right at that moment when another dog appeared on the other side of the pond and Wendell, seeing him, took off in a brisk run across the ice, and that's when everything went into slow-mo. Me and Carrie racing forward, our mouths cavernous and twisted as we were screaming "Wendell, nooooooooooo!" Thatcher's sweet expression of concern over her best friend's fate (either that or she was thinking that boy dogs were so stupid), and of course the camera panning slowly across the ice, which was starting to crack apart at his sudden movement. I'm not sure whether I could actually see Wendell's face as the ice broke open beneath him, but continuing with the movie analogy let's just say that I did, and his expression was that perfect sitcom look of "wait a second, something is not right here" and then *splash!* in he went into the icy, fast-moving current. (Okay, scratch that, there was no fast-moving current, it was a still pond, but still very icy.) Next, there was that millisecond of nothingness, as if Wendell had just gotten swallowed by the earth and had ceased to exist, and then he bobbed back up sputtering and dog-paddling like, well, like a dog in a freezing-cold pond.

Luckily the ice was thin enough to break up before him as he moved toward the edge that was closest to him, which of course was not an edge that he would be able to climb up and back onto dry land, but a two-foot embankment. Suddenly I was right there, throwing myself onto the muddy ground so I could make a human chain to reach him. (Okay, so it wasn't really a human chain, but Carrie was nearby and ready to throw herself down, too, if a human chain was needed.) As I reached out across the freakin' freezing water I was able to grab one of his front paws and I pulled him closer to the edge. I like to think that I was doing my best to keep him calm and saying things like "It's okay, honey, we're gonna get you out of there. Don't worry, you'll be fine" (oooh, what about the speech that Kate gives Jack in the final scene of *Titanic*, hmmmmm . . . I'll have to rent that again for future quotes), or "Mommy loves you and this hellish freak-show nightmare will soon be over and I'll have you home and under a warm blow dryer eating steak in no time." But what I was really saying (Carrie told me this later, but only after I made her) was something more along the line of "AHHHHHHHHHH!!" With a few sailor expletives thrown in for good measure.

Now I needed to figure out a way to heave his forty-seven-pound frame up onto dry land, which was going to be particularly tricky given the fact that I was notoriously lax at doing arm exercises at the gym. Sizing up the situation, I knew it was time for me to invoke the goddess of super-human strength for moms in extenuating situations, the same goddess that grants that special burst of strength to women who have to lift SUVs off the limbs of their children or have to break down steel doors in order to save their child from some bad guy, and I wavered for only a tiny moment, as I was trying to remember whether there was a limit to such times you can ask for help because I knew damn well that there would probably be plenty more times where I might need a bit of help and I certainly didn't know if I wanted to use up my one chance on this particular situation, as I could conceivably just jump into the pond and heave him up to shore myself. But I decided that any reasonable goddess would probably look at every situation on a case-by-case basis and that it never hurts to just ask.

So gripping Wendell under the armpits (if that's what they are called on dogs) of his front legs I managed to heave him vertically up in the air and out of the water and finally by whipping my body to the right I soon had a very wet, cold, and dirty dog on my chest. I remember staring up at the sky, blinking and gasping (I couldn't breathe with him on my chest), how he quickly scurried off me to go say hey to the new dog, and that I said a silent thank you to the patron saint of dog owners. After another minute or two Carrie's face was soon peering down at me. "Are you okay?"

I nodded, and gratefully took her outstretched hand. After she helped me up and we both marveled over the fact that there didn't appear to be any part of me that wasn't now covered in mud, we looked at each other and burst out laughing. Me, laughing at the whole situation, especially the part when I was the world's shallowest dog-mom by thinking only of my photo album as opposed to my own dog's safety. And Carrie, laughing at me.

I'm pleased to report that Wendell didn't seem to suffer any symptoms of post-traumatic stress disorder from the frozen-pond fiasco (though the interior of our car was a whole other matter). And I like to think that this is mainly because he never doubted for a second that I'd save him, because whether we were on the prairie or at a park in Cambridge I would always be there to watch after him and to protect him as best I could (and with the backup of good friends who had a cell phone handy).

How to Deal with a Sick Dog

When you find the weird bump, odd-shaped bruise, tiny cut, sketchy discharge, funny odor, or in this particular case, flat fleshy tumor that is located on the top of your dog's head, it will most certainly be at two minutes after six o'clock, which means that your vet's office is now closed. Decide to call anyway, on the off chance that someone is still there and feeling nice enough to answer the phone even though business hours are officially over. No such luck, so instead you get the answering service with a very bored operator who really doesn't give a rat's ass about the fact that you just found some sort of flat fleshy tumor on the top of your dog's head. Again and again, like a machine that will eventually replace her, the bored operator will keep responding to your increasingly frantic questions by reading off her little card that says in case of emergency patients should go to Angel Memorial Animal Hospital, which is open twenty-four hours, and she'd be happy to give me the number.

Against your better judgment ask her if *she's* ever heard of a flat fleshy tumor disease. She sighs, debating as to whether to ignore your question and just read off her little card again, but she decides to be honest and says no. Instantly feel better but the relief is short-lived as she follows up her no with a clause along the lines of "Not like I'd know, though, I don't even like dogs." Be offended and decide right then and there that you will write a letter to your veterinarian about the rude operator who answers his phone on off hours and the fact that she doesn't even like dogs. Realize that you forgot to ask for her name and swear.

Go and grab one of the three different dog-health guides that you own and start frantically paging through it while trying to figure out what the flat fleshy tumor disease would be called so you can look it up in the index. Wonder why medical books can't just list symptoms and then tell you every disease that you could have based on said symptoms. Decide that mass hysteria would not be good. Remember that most medical diseases have Latin origins and then swear again about your lack of foresight when dropping Latin your sophomore year of college because the class started too early. Take the Pepé Le Pew approach (meaning that one can speak French by placing the prefix le before every word) and add in the Latin sounding icus at the end of each word and begin looking for a listing of *Flatticus Fleshicus Tumorosiosis*. Find nothing. Instead, read about other dog diseases for a while just to further fan the flames of what's becoming a full-scale panic attack. Finally, push aside books in disgust and swear three times in quick succession.

Go to your laptop and quickly Google search "flat fleshy tumor and dogs" while chanting "Please don't let anything come up. Please don't let anything come up." But of course

this *is* the Internet we are talking about, so 476 links come up
that contain the words *flat, fleshy, tumor,* and *dog.* Titter
nervously to yourself as you scan the various links until you
get to the page that talks about malignant histiocytomas,
which is a dog disease that entails an undefined and fleshy
type of tumor that is normally cancerous. Breathe in ragged
gasps as your eyes do the fifty-yard dash all the way down the
page. You are one step away from an asthma attack (even
though you don't have asthma) when you find out that such
tumors may arise from any anatomic site in the body (like
the top of the head, where you found the one on your dog),
sarcomas spread through the blood in up to 25 percent of
cases, local recurrence blah blah poor response to chemother-
apy blah blah, which can be boiled down to start practicing
your eulogy now.

Never mind that most dog breeds have never had an oc-
currence of the disease, the two exceptions being the Bernese
mountain dog and the flat-coated retriever, both of which
your dog happens not to be, but you know that there is no
such thing as never. Put your face in your hands and say,
"Dammit, dammit all to hell."

When your husband comes home an hour later he finds
the dog resting on a mountain of pillows in bed, having been
fed the chicken that was earlier that day designated for his
own dinner. Husband is no dummy and realizes that something is amiss but isn't quite sure whether or not he wants
to get dragged into the middle of whatever it is that is

allowing the dog to get fed his dinner. He goes through the possibilities:

1. Wife is mad at husband and decides to give the dog husband's dinner.

2. Wife loves dog more than husband and decides to give the dog husband's dinner.

3. Wife realizes we are out of dogfood and decides to give the dog husband's dinner.

4. Wife has somehow found out that the husband is dying and decides not to waste the "good stuff" on him and gives the dog husband's dinner.

Before he gets to number five, wail out the reason that the dog is getting the chicken instead of him. Tell him that the dog is dying from a rare flat fleshy tumor disease. Pound your fists into his chest, wipe your snotty nose on his shirt, and cry uncontrollably while repeating over and over that the prognosis is generally considered to be poor. Husband lets you cry it out for a while, hoping you'll tire out and be easier to manage (learned this trick in dealing with the dog), and twenty minutes later you are all puffy-faced but docile as a newborn deer sitting meekly by your husband on the couch where you show him the link that says your dog is as good as dead.

Husband is rolling eyes and swearing under his breath, as he is a medical doctor himself and has to deal with hysteria and misinformation all the time when patients with overzealous Type A personalities come in for their appointment after doing a "little research" on the Web, and he says that he would like to check it out himself.

Meanwhile, puppy is feeling fat and full of chicken as he lazes about on the bed in front of the air conditioner, which is turned on even though it's fifty degrees out, as an extra-special treat (he likes air blowing in his face). Show your husband that area directly on the top of his head where it should just be furry skin pulled tight over his darling little skull, but instead it's sort of flat and fleshy and you can press your fingers inward about two or three millimeters.

Finally, after much stroking, prodding, pushing, and poking, your husband tells you that whatever it is that you are thinking is a flat fleshy tumor is in fact not one at all. Demand an explanation while grabbing your husband's hand and letting him push down on the top of your own head that is just scalp and bone, then flip his hand over knuckle-side down and rap his hand on your head to show you that it is hard as a rock, and there is no soft fleshy spot to be found. Move his hand over to rap the dog's head for comparison, but before you can do this he jerks his hand away. Your dog is confused and is looking back and forth at you both expectantly, wishing you would hurry up and give him a cookie already. Go get the dog a cookie and call out over your shoulder and ask what that flat fleshy tumorlike patch *is* then, if he's so damn smart?

Your husband waits until you return and after your dog has had his cookie. He then gently takes both of your hands and places them on your dog's ears and then slowly moves both hands toward each other and the center of your dog's head. Hmmmm, it seems that your husband's theory is that the fleshy area on top of his head is probably made up of stuff that actually keeps his ears attached to his head—like a ligament or perhaps even the muscle that is used to move his ears forward and backward in that cute way he does whenever he hears some funny noise.

After a moment of rapid blinking, buy what your husband is selling, as it does seem pretty logical, since there is no other place for ear-movement muscles to lie on your dog's head (you check, of course) and you are feeling very much relieved and grateful to your husband for saving the life of your dog. Stand arm in arm for a few moments longer watching as the air conditioner blows out cold air right in your dog's face and comment how his hair looks almost like wheat swaying in the wind. (Well, at least the version of wheat fields the media has shown us, which is apparently inaccurate as wheat growing is actually green. But know that even if your dog were green like wheat you'd love him just as much.) Your husband kisses the top of your head and then asks whether there is anything left for dinner.

FOR WHOM THE TAGS JINGLE

I saw the sign as I was on the way to the grocery store; tacked onto a community bulletin board front-and-center was the one word that could strike fear into the heart of any dog owner—*LOST*. Below the word was a picture of a black-and-white dog that obviously loved the camera (or more likely, the person behind it), as his tail was one big blur of happiness. Below the picture, written in all caps, was the word *BUDDY* and a brief description: "three years old, black-and-white mixed-breed dog, fifty pounds, with a blue collar that has identification tags." Below that, written in red, was *BIG REWARD*, accented with an entire row of dollar signs $$$$$$$$$$$$$$$ and exclamation points !!!!!!!!! At the very bottom of the page, most likely written by the brokenhearted child of the family, was this last cry for help: "Buddy likes tennis balls and peanut butter."

Horrified, my hand over my mouth, I realized I was holding my breath, and when I exhaled I whispered to myself, "Wendell likes tennis balls and peanut butter, too." And with that I sprinted back to the car, and was soon on my way to Petco.

I stood in front of the machine that made customized dog tags, staring at the selection of tags that I was to choose from—small round silver circle, large silver circle, silver dog-bone shape, silver fire hydrant (what's with this whole fire-hydrant dog thing? As if I'd pick an object that dogs peed on to represent my dog's identity), gold circle, and red heart. I had already put in my tokens and now just had to pick, but I was trying to decide between the large silver circle and the red heart. The silver circle matched the best with his red collar with its silver buckle, but of course the heart is the international symbol for love and perhaps if someone found Wendell they would see that little heart-shaped tag and know that he was truly loved and the fact that he was lost was obviously some horrible mistake and that his owner was no doubt in hysterics roaming the streets looking for him this very moment so they had better call fast as she would surely die of grief if he was not returned in a timely manner.

I pushed the button below the red heart, and watched as the mechanical arms moved it to the center, ready to be engraved. Next I had to figure out what I was going to say. Being a fast typist, I immediately dashed out the words "If you are reading this then you obviously have my dog and if you don't bring him back I will hunt you down for all eternity." I looked at the screen once finished and saw that only the first twelve letters of my threat were there, "If you are r." Twelve lousy characters, that was all I got? HOW ABSURD! WHO COULD POSSIBLY CONVEY ANYTHING WITH TWELVE STUPID CHARACTERS?!

I scanned the directions on the right and saw that I got another two lines. OH PLEASE! LIKE THIRTY-SIX CHARACTERS IS EVEN THAT MUCH BETTER. I MEAN, WHAT IF SOMEONE GAVE SHAKE-SPEARE ONLY THIRTY-SIX CHARACTERS? OR TOLSTOY? OR JANE AUSTEN!!!

I tried again while muttering under my breath.

> If you are r
> eading this
> then you obv

Okay, so I needed to refine my message. I cleared the screen to start again.

> I will pay y
> ou so much m
> oney you can

Okay, hopefully the third time's the charm, and I decided that the nice-guy approach would probably be better than a threat of bodily harm.

> Please pleas
> Call me I am
> Begging you!

Now, would someone find this message with the misspelled second *please* charming or just desperate? Maybe they would think that Wendell was better off with them versus a woman who couldn't spell and was not above begging.

> Pleaseplease
> PleasePlease
> PleasePlease

Okay, so I was obviously not begging, but it still wasn't right, though I did give myself a mental pat on the back for being smart enough to omit the spaces as needed. My fifth attempt was a little better.

> PleasePlease
> Imissmymom
> Callhernow!!

Just as I was about to hit "enter" to engrave away I realized that I didn't include a phone number. I pressed the enter button and decided that I would just make another tag that would include a number. I picked the large silver circle.

> 617–555–0679
> 617–555–7777
> CallCallCall

The third tag (gold circle) said in all caps (DAMMIT WHY HADN'T I THOUGHT OF USING ALL CAPS BEFORE!):

> THE REWARD 4
> ME IS HUGE
> U R RICH NOW

Ugh, this one was stupid, and so I tried again.

BIG!BIG!BIG!
LIKE,HUGE
REWARD 4 ME

Right as I printed that one I realized that I never gave
Wendell's name and our address (because what if they didn't
have a cell phone, or a quarter, or access to anyplace that had
a phone?).

MY NAME IS
WENDELL
12WENDELLST.

Too hard to understand.

WENDELL of
12 WENDELL
STREET MA

I now regretted that we lived on Wendell Street, as it made
everything quite confusing. I tapped the glass nervously.
"Think, Jenny, think." I did the next two tags (another red
heart and the gold circle) in quick succession, pressing buttons like a pro.

MY NAME IS
WENDELL
I AM ONLY 2

> 12Wendell St
> Cambridge MA
> Named for St (I added this last bit just in case they
> were wondering.)

I now held in my hand six new tags and I was sweating. I read
through them all and racked my brain to see if there was anything I had forgotten. I stared at the display and realized that
the only tag I had not utilized was the fire-hydrant one. I
wondered whether it was bad luck that I didn't use them all,
as if using one of each might prove to be the winning combination. What the hell, what's another three bucks for a little
more peace of mind?

I deliberated on the last one for a while, as I wanted it to
be my grand finale, my encore—a final summation of love,
hope, fear, and true desperation. This one had to be the
clincher, the closer, the one thing that would warm the heart
of even the meanest, angriest, most despicable person on the
face of the planet.

> IF YOU CAN'T
> RETURN ME
> THEN LOVE ME

HA! TAKE THAT! YOU'D HAVE TO HAVE A
HEART OF STONE OR BETTER YET SOME-
THING EVEN HARDER THAN STONE—
SOMETHING THAT WAS THE HARDEST

SUBSTANCE ON EARTH, EVEN, TO RESIST THAT ONE.

I left the store feeling triumphant, but knowing that my work was not yet done. I thought about the fact that in any missing-person case, or in my case, a missing dog, time was of utmost importance. With every hour that passed, the odds of getting back a loved one would begin to drop (hey, I watch *Without a Trace*), and I was nothing if not efficient. I drove directly to my local Staples, where I bought poster board, a ream of paper, a lamination kit, colored markers, three staple guns, a set of walkie-talkies (communication is key when it comes to missing persons), and talked to the manager about where I might be able to find a bullhorn. (He didn't know, but seemed relieved when I left the store.)

When I got home I cleared the kitchen table and got started designing LOST DOG posters, leaving enough room to add the pictures in later, as I had plans to take new photos of Wendell from every angle—Wendell sitting, Wendell standing, Wendell from the right profile, Wendell from the left (which was his best side), Wendell from the back, and maybe even an aerial shot of him as well (for the search planes and news helicopters). I thought about whether he had any distinguishing features (besides the fact that he was the cutest dog alive) and was dismayed after much searching to find that he didn't have any birthmarks. I made a few phone calls and found a tattoo parlor that was willing to tattoo him if I brought in a note from my veterinarian and my therapist (hmmm, wonder how they knew I'd have one?). I decided that the best tattoo for Wendell would be a heart with the word *Mommy* on it and that I would perhaps get a matching one that said *Wendell* so I could prove that we were a pair. I then dropped the tattoo idea as I remembered that tattoos were incredibly painful and wondered if I should use a red Sharpie pen to color a lock of his hair since dogs were color-blind and so none of his friends would even be able to notice it and make fun of him (I could take care of any humans who dared to remark on it).

Cosmas came home hours later to find me sitting on our couch talking into our video camera, which I had set up on a tripod. I signaled him to not say anything and out of my peripheral vision I saw him standing in the doorway watching me as I read the speech that I had written and memorized.

"Hello. My name is Jenny Lee and I am talking to you today about my lost dog, whose name is *Wendell*." I held up a close-up picture of Wendell's face. "*Wendell* is a wheaten terrier. *Wendell* is twenty inches tall and weighs approximately forty-five pounds." I held up a side-view picture of Wendell. "*Wendell* has honey-wheat blond hair and is very fuzzy but with no visible tangles. *Wendell* is a very happy dog and is very much loved and missed. *Wendell* likes to play tug-of-war but we discourage this game, as he gets a little rambunctious. *Wendell* loves Kraft Singles"—I held up a cheese slice, which I knew might be too over-the-top, but figured I could edit it out later—"whipped cream, and strawberry ice cream. *Wendell* has a red collar with six identification tags that have our phone number, address, and also discuss the fact that we are willing to pay a huge sum of money for any information on his whereabouts and then we'll pay even more for his safe return. *Wendell* is only two years old and really needs to be with us as he is a little klutzy and is prone to anxiety attacks. We, me and my husband"—at this point I held up a framed picture of the three of us that was taken a few months ago at the beach—"love and adore *Wendell* and want him back more than anything else in the world. So if you see *Wendell* or have seen any dog fitting his description, please call the toll-free action hot line that we have set up, 1–800–W–E–N–D–E–L–L, please call as operators are standing by." I was pretty sure that was it but checked the cue card in my lap to make sure and saw that I had written the direction "Now start to cry." And on cue I started to cry, sobbing into my hands for full effect, and wondering if it would be even better if I pretended to faint, but then decided against it in case someone thought I dropped dead and then wouldn't return him now that I looked like I was dead.

I got up to turn off the camera, but quickly changed my mind and sat back down again, faced the camera, and in my best Mel Gibson (from the movie *Ransom*) imitation I screamed into the camera, "GIVE ME BACK MY DOG, YOU SICK, DERANGED LUNATIC BECAUSE IF YOU DON'T I SWEAR YOU WILL SPEND THE REST OF YOUR DAYS LOOKING OVER YOUR SHOULDER AND LIVING IN FEAR THAT I WILL ONE DAY CATCH UP WITH YOU AND BELIEVE

YOU ME, JACKO, I WILL FIND YOU AND MAKE YOU SORRY. YOU HAVE MESSED WITH THE WRONG FAMILY. DO YOU UNDERSTAND ME?!!!"

This was when Cosmas walked over to me, blocking my shot. I started to protest but when I looked up at Cosmas he had a look on his face that I had never seen before, which could only be described as a combination of wonderment and fear.

I blinked rapidly and wiped my nose with the back of my hand.

"What on earth are you doing screaming into the camera like that? Have you lost your mind? Wendell is right behind you." And with that he pointed to Wendell, who was looking a little freaked out and was hovering in the little nook between the couch and the bookshelf (his safe place). As I stared at Wendell he cocked his head to the left, which is what he does when he's confused (to the right meant he was just hamming it up and hoping for a treat), and I leapt out of the chair and rushed for him, scooping him up in my arms as I plopped down on the couch and buried my face in his fur. (Drats. I forgot to say that Wendell smelled good. I'll have to do another take later.)

Moments later I felt a finger tapping me on the shoulder and when I looked up Cosmas was squatting before me with a different look on his face.

"Is this about that other dog, Buddy?"

My eyes grew wide. "How do you know about Buddy?"

In a soft voice, he said, "There was a poster near work and when I saw it I thought about Wendell, too." Which is when he produced a single dog tag (red heart) that read:

> WENDELL
> 617–555–0679
> Cambridge, MA

So simple, so perfect, and completely summing up everything that needed to be said (well, except the huge reward that we'd mortgage everything we owned to provide). This is when I poured out the whole story of my day, how I saw the sign at the grocery store (oops, forgot to buy food for dinner), how I spazzed out and went straight to Petco to make him a tag, how I had a meltdown at the machine over what to say (as I've never been spare with words) and ended up making six tags, and how I went to Staples, and about my sketches for the posters and signs, my emergency contingency Excel spreadsheet complete with phone tree, and the fact that I really had no idea where to buy a bullhorn, but I just knew that if I could find one then everything would be okay, as if I could just be loud enough about my love for Wendell then he'd be safe forever.

Cosmas gave me a little Phew!-thank-God-I-don't-have- any- estrogen- because- you're- crazy- but- you're- my-crazy shoulder squeeze, and assured me that by the sound of my day my love for Wendell was coming out loud and clear even without a bullhorn.

I had obviously been squeezing Wendell a little too tightly and he chose that time to wiggle free, and he jumped down to the floor and started to walk toward the kitchen (intense affection made him thirsty). It was then that I heard the jingling sound of six crazy tags (soon to be seven) clanging together. Cosmas and I laughed at the sound, which was plenty loud.

The 10 Breeds of Obsessed Dog Owners

9. The Owner Who Would Be Dog

This dog owner seems a little too in tune with his dog, if you know what I mean. He has no problem getting on all fours and barking at his dog. He says things like, "I don't know what it is, but most dogs just seem to love me." He will then proceed to maul your dog with all sorts of pats and hugs and rubs that your dog clearly doesn't enjoy. When your dog tries to jump on him and you try to stop him (as you do not want a dog who jumps on people), he encourages it by patting his thighs and saying, "I don't mind—it's what dogs like to do." These people are not above feeding dogs food out of their own mouths; they will have mastered many different barks and whines; and it becomes clear they wish they had tails too. They'll probably tell you they think they were dogs in a former life. To which you can only nod and say, "How lovely." Just to be on the safe side, you will want to back away from them slowly. After all, it's one thing for a dog to try humping a person's leg, but . . .

10

Do All Holidays Now Revolve Around Your Dog?

HOW TO CELEBRATE HALLOWEEN WITH YOUR DOG

You have always been against dressing up dogs. Sure you've done the bandanna thing; you may have even gone so far as to buy Mickey Mouse ears for your dog at Disneyland (of course, that was strictly for a photo op). You also had to admit that the other day when you saw a woman walking a boxer that was wearing a strand of pearls, you thought it looked nice. But you draw the line when it comes to making your dog wear entire outfits. Tutus? Humiliating. Tuxedos? Please! Sweater and matching kilt? As if!

Given all this, you are quite surprised when you find yourself standing in the center aisle of Petco transfixed by all the different Halloween costumes they have for dogs. The first thought in your head, of course, is *Halloween costumes for dogs? Preposterous!* —okay, maybe your *first* thought is that the jack-o'-lantern number pictured on the Westie is, like, beyond cute—and you will yourself to walk away. But that's when you notice that the cowboy costume comes with a little holster and two six-shooters (love it!).

Continue walking down the aisle while trying to remember what it is you were supposed to be looking for and as you do this your head begins to fill with images of the Halloween costumes you wore in your own youth—the ladybug, the princess, and that time you were supposed to be a big red crayon but everyone kept thinking you were a hot dog. Smile at these memories and remember how much you love Halloween, and that it was actually your third-favorite holiday after Christmas and your own birthday. Breathe deeply thinking of the crisp fall nights when your parents treated you like a baby and made you wear a coat over your costume (c'mon, what self-respecting penguin would be caught dead in a bright green down jacket?), the giddy anticipation of running up to the next house on the street, and the divine weight of your pillowcase getting heavier and heavier with loot.

This is when you realize that this is your dog's *first* Halloween (read: major photo op for the record you're keeping of "firsts" in his life) and that in human years he is only seven years old, which means that he's just a kid (and c'mon, what kind of parent would ever deprive a seven-year-old of the joys of Halloween?). So then you rationalize to yourself that letting your dog celebrate a Halloween or two by dressing up would probably be fine when he is only a year or two old, and that obviously when he is a more mature dog and in dog years older than yourself you won't make him dress up at all (well, not unless he wants to).

You are now once again standing in front of the Halloween costumes and you are trying to find a jack-o'-lantern in medium. When you do find one, open it up and check out the fabric (orange fuzzy velour) and laugh out loud when you see the little hat with the stem on top. Know that your dog will be the best damn jack-o'-lantern anyone has ever seen.

Rush home with your purchase, calling your husband from the car to ask him what he thinks about dressing up the dog for Halloween, and there is something in your voice that makes him know that you are asking him this even though you have already bought a costume, so he quickly agrees that Halloween is certainly a holiday that should be shared by small children and young dogs alike. This makes you happy and you decide to wait until later to show off the costume.

Now at home your dog is happy to see you and seems to know that you have just come home from Petco and so he sits in front of you patiently awaiting the newest addition to his toy chest. Give him a friendly rub and show him the stuffed Frankenstein toy that you got him, which he immediately slams down to the ground and rolls on his back to play dead (his best trick). You toss the toy in the air and he flips upright and springs, catching it in midair, and the toy makes a *dum dum dum dum, dum dum dum dum duuuuuum* noise. Clap your hands in glee as your baby bucks like a bronco with sheer delight.

Later that night after your husband gets home you graciously allow him to eat dinner before staging the holiday fashion show. But no sooner than he puts his fork down, you leap out of your chair, almost knocking it over, and cause your dog to leap to his own paws and start barking like crazy. Your dog's excitement only grows as you pull out the Petco bag from the closet (could he have already begun reading?) and you pull out his Halloween costume. Your husband's face crinkles up like a raisin, as he must have been hoping for a more macho costume for your dog (say the Terminator?), so then let him know that he can pick out next year's costume. (Ignore him when he points out that you mentioned that it was only going to be this year that you dressed him up.)

At the sight of the orange fuzzy thing, your dog goes ballistic and is doing that thing where he is running through all the tricks he knows—sitting, throwing both paws up for a shake and then a high-five, and then he slams down on the floor, does a full rollover, and plays dead. Obviously your dog is in for a rude awakening, at which time you throw yourself on the dog (some might call this a sucker-punch move) and begin to force him into the costume, which encircles his entire body and his two front legs. You have to pin the thrashing jack-o'-lantern onto the ground in order to Velcro the costume closed and finally you are done and you release him.

Your dog goes literally insane; he is hurling himself to the ground as if the Grim Reaper himself were on his back and making a sound that is borderline scary. You run to the cookie jar hoping to distract him with food, but he's not interested. You up the ante by going to the fridge and grabbing a Kraft Singles and still he's not interested (this freaks you out a bit, as the only thing left that is better than cheese is ice cream, of which you have none).

By now your husband is up on his feet commanding you to take the costume off the dog and he's doing it in a bellowing voice and pointing his finger, first at you and then at the dog. Move to do so, but now your dog wants nothing to do with you, as he knows it was you who did this to him in the first place. Finally you corner him and then take off the costume and you suddenly feel a wave of regret for traumatizing him so, but this is of course coupled with the fact that you are annoyed that you didn't have the foresight to take a picture of him while you had the chance.

Now that your dog is free of the costume he promptly ices you out and runs for your husband and you are left with a crumpled costume, wondering whether you kept the receipt as you are now going to have to find something else.

Over the next week you try several different costumes and your dog reacts more or less the same to everything else (dinosaur, devil, bumblebee) and you are about to give up hope when you find a pair of small angel wings that comes with a halo hat. The wings are small enough so that he isn't able to reach back and rip them off and the hat is a no go, but hey, at this point you're willing to take any photo op you can get.

Swear that this is the last Halloween that you will be dressing up your dog, but renege on this as soon as you hear everyone cooing with delight upon seeing your sweet little angel walking, almost floating, next to you. 🐾

WHAT WENDELL WANTS

When Wendell flips over his water bowl, I know he wants more water. When Wendell lies next to me while I'm eating at the table, I know he wants some of my food. When Wendell stands directly in my field of vision when I'm watching TV and barks, I first try to avoid eye contact, but eventually get worn down, as I know that he wants one of three things—he wants to go outside because he needs to use the bathroom, he wants to go outside because he heard another dog outside and wants to go play, or he wants me to pay attention to him, as I'm obviously not doing anything important (Wendell doesn't quite get the appeal of TV).

Of course, there are plenty of times when I don't know what he wants. I don't know what he wants when he lies on his chair and stares at me and sighs. Sometimes I wonder if he's doing that cartoon thing and is simply hungry and looking at me like I'm a giant Chicken McNugget or perhaps a giant boiled egg. I have no idea what he wants when he lies on the couch in my office and simply stares at my bookshelves. Does he wish he could read? Sometimes I spend hours attending to not just the basic wants of his life, but also the big-picture wants of his life. Does he wish he had opposable paws? Does he wish he had a patch of grass to call his own? Does he wish that he had different parents, lived on the West Coast, perhaps on a farm where he could chase all interesting sorts of livestock?

Yes, I know these thoughts are idle, as there are some things about my dog I'll probably never crack. But you have to give it the old college try, right?

One night Cosmas came home from work to find me lying on the rug next to Wendell, trying to press his right paw into an inkpad. Some people would find this odd, mind you, but not Cosmas, who now had a pretty high shock tolerance when it came to my relationship with Wendell. He just walked over, squatted next to me, kissed me on the head, and told me that he didn't think that paw prints were the same as fingerprints, and then he asked me whether I *had* to carry out this project right on our new rug. Sheepishly, I gathered up the paper that was scattered about and pointed out that I had been using newspaper as a blotter just in case.

While I was thus occupied, Wendell ran over to Cosmas and proceeded to stamp his new khakis with two perfect paw prints on the upper thighs—one red, one green. Cosmas gave Wendell a friendly rub, saving his grimace of annoyance for me, and motioned toward his pants in marital sign language saying, "Now look at what've you done." I offered a few half-hearted *tsks* of the tongue by way of apology, but then gave him a big smile. Nothing could ruin my good mood tonight. With both hands I held up a large white envelope that was now decorated and did a little dance, which made Wendell, who had only just settled in his chair, leap back up in excitement (he loved to dance).

Cosmas took the envelope from my hands, inspected the address label, and then looked up at me with a look of total shock (ha, I've still got it). He opened his mouth to speak, but I quickly shushed him with some sign language of my own, you know that elementary-school move of locking your mouth with an imaginary key. I even tossed it over my shoulder, with dramatic flair. I motioned to Wendell, who was now standing equidistantly between us, looking first to me and then to Cosmas, as if he knew we were talking about him, and then I mouthed the word *later*.

An hour later Wendell had had his last walk of the evening, Cosmas had eaten two-thirds of a PB&J (need you ask who got the rest of it?), and we were now ensconced in bed, three peas in a pod. As much as we try to get Wendell to sleep in between us after playing rock paper scissors to see what direction we spoon, he always gets up and walks down to the foot of the bed, where he leans up against the footboard facing toward the air conditioner (maybe Wendell just wants to know how to turn on the AC). And tonight, after he'd settled in his usual spot, I quickly sat up, turned on the bedside lamp, and whipped out the envelope from underneath my pillow. Seeing the envelope, Cosmas quickly lifted up my pillows and scowled at the two faint paw prints now stamped on the sheet. Oops.

I shrugged it off and mumbled something about our linens now matching his pants. I mean, how could he be worrying about our sheets, when I was about to reveal the contents of the package?

I handed it to Cosmas and he took it gingerly in his fingertips (he had a bizarre bad experience in elementary school and now has a weird aversion to ink on skin—believe me, don't ask).

Still pissy about the sheets, Cosmas whispered, "You know, Christmas is still weeks away."

I displayed my best pouty face in response and grabbed for the envelope, not wanting him to ever see it if he was going to be such a grump about the whole thing. He held the envelope over his head out of the reach of my arms, though, and his face began to soften, mainly because he didn't want to get into it with me before bed (he was a guy who needed his eight hours), and also because he *was* human after all and honestly, who could be a grinch when it came to your dog's first letter to Santa?

His mood now somewhat improved, Cosmas now took a good look at the envelope Wendell and I had spent most of the day decorating—the tree that was fashioned out of smudged green paw prints, the individual red paw prints that

I used for ornaments, and finally the intricate (albeit abstract) portrait of the addressee in question that was depicted on the verso. He pointed toward the address, curious to know how I had managed to track down Santa's official address, and he nodded when I told him that the Internet was good for a few things. I then explained that I was already worried that we were sending it on the late side, as I knew it had to be important to not get lost in the shuffle, but I reasoned that once Santa saw how much effort had gone into our packaging maybe he'd overlook the fact that Wendell was a dog.

Cosmas nodded slowly at this, apparently tired enough to find himself agreeing with my rationale.

Opening the folded letter, Cosmas gasped at the stationery we had fashioned—the faded green paw-print wreath with its paw red bow adorning the top. I explained that it had taken over five tries to get one really good wreath and that I had made each of the other five pages by pressing them into the ink and then using a paper towel and a blow dryer to get the finished product. I couldn't quite tell whether Cosmas was still impressed by the artistic side of his wife and dog (Martha Stewart, eat your heart out) or was just freaking out over the fact that the damn thing was five pages long.

Before he could make any cracks about Wendell's penmanship, I explained that I had written the letter myself, obviously, though I was certain it was written exactly how Wendell wanted it. It read as follows:

Dear Santa, Ms. Santa, Merry Elves, and the loyal dogs of the North Pole:

My name is Wendell and I will be two years and three months and four days old by Christmas Day. This is my first letter to you, as last year I was just a young pup and didn't feel quite up to the task of expressing myself through a letter, but as you may remember I did sit on your lap when you visited the Petco in Cambridge, Massachusetts. (I'm enclosing a picture of us together, as I know you must meet lots of dogs throughout the year.)

I am writing this letter at the suggestion of my mommy, who told me all about how you and your family live in the North Pole. Perhaps I can come and visit you one day, as I really like the snow and have lots of hair to keep me warm. I would like to meet your reindeer; do they like dogs? Anyway, she also told me that you get a lot of letters from human kids every year where they tell you what they would like for Christmas, and when I asked her whether you got any letters from dogs she said that you probably did, but not that many. In view of this, I decided that I would write to you not only for myself, but also on behalf of all the dogs I know.

I suppose I should get to the point (as I know you must be very busy this time of year) and tell you what I really want for Christmas. I feel a little shy about asking for things outright like this, as I was not raised to be a rude dog, but apparently this is the point of these letters. (Though I promise to write you again in the off-season just to show you that I will continue to care about you even after the payoff . . . I mean, your big day.)

I'm not sure how many things I'm supposed to ask for, but I'll defer to the standard rule of contractual negotiation and ask for more things than I need in hopes that your counteroffer will be fair.

I would like a yard that has a fence so I could sit outside on my own sometimes. Sure I like having my mommy around, but sometimes she gets busy and I feel like I get gypped out of "outside time." I promise to share my yard with my other doggy friends.

I would like a new squeaky ball, one that is not too hard but not too soft.

I would like a gift certificate to Toscanini's Ice Cream in Cambridge (you should really try to stop by there en route and sample their oatmeal-raisin-cookie ice cream).

I want to go to the big park more—not the big park in the sky, mind you, but the one with the pond by the railroad tracks. It would also be great if it didn't rain so much (not sure if that's something you can take care of, but maybe you could put in a good word).

I want a bigger chair—I just feel like I've outgrown mine a bit, and though it's still comfy, I feel like I need a bit more room. (I promise to give my old chair to a dog less fortunate than myself.)

I want some more rawhides, but this is not all that important as my mommy seems to always have some.

I don't want to take any more baths (not sure if you can control the "don't wants," but I figured it doesn't hurt to ask).

And what I want the most, more than anything in the world—so much so that if I get this one gift I don't need anything else—I would like to have my own dog. Mommy says that I probably have a snowball's chance in hell of getting this since my daddy is totally against getting a second dog, but I thought I'd ask anyway (by the way, do you know why you can't make snowballs in hell? Where is hell?).

I promise that I will totally take care of the dog myself—he can walk when I walk and I will even share all my food and toys (though I don't know if I can share my chair since I barely fit in it alone, as it is). I guess the reason that I want a dog is because sometimes I think it'd be nice to have someone more like me to hang out with—Mommy is cool and all, but it's just not the same.

Well, that's all I have to say right now. Thanks so much for your time and consideration of all my requests. I would also like to say that I've been a pretty good dog this year, not perfect of course (there was a mud-puddle incident that I'm not proud of), but as good as I can be.

Please say hi to everyone there, especially your own dog. What's his name?

Respectfully and sincerely yours,
Wendell Elvis Giallourakis
Of Wendell Street in Cambridge, MA

Being a slow reader, Cosmas finished reading the letter well after I did (obviously I had read it several times already, but can I just say that even in the fifth reading I was still moved by this young pup's sense of wonderment—I mean, how cute that he asked to meet Santa's reindeer!), but as I watched my husband slowly fold the letter back up and replace it in the envelope, I could tell that he wasn't quite as moved by it as I was. Actually, he seemed pretty pissed.

"You do know that it's really not cool of you to do this."

"Do what?" Immediately on the defensive, I asked, "What are you talking about? It's just a letter from Wendell to Santa."

At the mention of his name, Wendell popped up his sleepy head and looked over at us. As if on cue, Cosmas and I both waved him back to sleep. After Wendell put his head down and we both had given him another round of goodnight kisses, we resumed our conversation, but this time we whispered.

"Look, why are you so mad?"

"I'm not mad about the letter, per se, but it's not nice to use . . ."—Cosmas paused and looked over at Wendell—"him, to further your own agenda."

"Agenda? Agenda? First of all, somebody's been watching *The West Wing* too much. But I didn't have an 'agenda' when I wrote that letter. It was supposed to be cute, that's all. I mean, don't you think I captured his personality?"

Annoyed at my *West Wing* comment as well as the fact that he assumed my personality question was just a trap to make him look like the bad guy (so what if it was?), Cosmas refused to go there. "Stop trying to change the subject. I said that this wasn't *about* the letter."

Now I was getting kind of upset myself, having spent the better part of a day working on this festive casus belli. "So what's the issue?"

"The issue is we are *not* getting another dog."

Ah, so *that* was the issue. I guess Cosmas did have a point, as I had been on his case lately, hinting that Wendell would really be happy to have someone to play with, though each time this was mentioned I was immediately shut down. So thereby having "Wendell" ask for a dog—and not even directly, but via the *cutest* letter in the world to Santa—well, I guess that could seem somewhat manipulative. Hmmm . . .

"Oh for Pete's sake, that was not the point of the letter!" (When you have no clear defense, there's always denial.)

"Oh really? So the point of the letter was not to ask for 'what I want most, more than anything in the world—so much so that if I get this one gift I don't need anything else . . .' Have you no *shame?*"

Taken aback by the fact that Cosmas actually was able to remember the passage almost verbatim, I just shrugged. "Nope. No shame. And I really think this whole thing has been blown *way* out of proportion. Let's just forget the whole thing."

The only thing Cosmas hated more than my playing the calculating wife was when I played the innocent. "So that's it? End of discussion?"

I shrugged and told him that, yes, it was the end of the discussion. Though it might get brought up again at the end of the month when Wendell woke up to find that Santa hadn't honored his wishes. I was joking of course, but Cosmas didn't find this remotely funny and was now storming out of bed, waking Wendell in the process. In one sudden motion Cosmas had scooped Wendell up into his arms and exited the bedroom. A moment later he was back in our room, sans Wendell, and quickly grabbed a pillow and an extra blanket off the bed.

I was dumbfounded, of course. I mean, who was being the juvenile here? Who knew that procrastination over doing laundry, a few inkpads, and some childlike handwriting could result in such complete and utter chaos? As I sat in bed listening to Cosmas removing the back sofa cushions to make more room on the couch, I tried to do a bit of soul-searching to see whether Wendell's letter to Santa was indeed just calculated brilliance on my part, or at least partially innocent.

Obviously it was a bit of a joke (though I had every intention of mailing the letter), but no more so than when Wendell and I took a road trip down to visit my friend Stephanie in Maryland and I sent postcards to Cosmas from Wendell. Or what about the fact that on Cosmas's birthday I got him an extra card and present from Wendell? Or what about the time that Wendell mailed Cosmas a cutout of a funny dog cartoon from *The New Yorker?* I mean, obviously a precedent had been set, as you could see a serial of behavior over a specific amount of time.

Armed with my new defense I got out of bed and walked into the dark living room and found Cosmas lying on his back with Wendell on his chest (yeah, like that would last long). I walked over to the couch and climbed up to sit on the armrest and now had my feet resting near Cosmas's head and I looked down between my legs at my husband, who was childish enough to pretend that he was still asleep.

"I object," I said.

"On what grounds?" he asked, eyes still closed.

"I object to having you sleeping on the couch on the grounds . . ."—I sighed, as I despised giving in, especially when at fault—"that perhaps my, or rather Wendell's . . ."—Cosmas opened one eye, and I continued—"fine, that my letter to Santa *from* Wendell was a tiny itty-bitty bit manipulative and unfair. *But* let the record show that such intent was done only because I really and truly believe"—I put my hand over my heart, but immediately felt stupid, as I was mixing up my gestures—"that this *is* what Wendell wants. I mean sure I wouldn't mind having a second dog, but I'm happy with just one. I think it's *Wendell* who would really benefit from it, and I, I . . ."

Cosmas finished my sentence for me. "You just want to make him happy." After saying this he put his arms around Wendell and sat up, letting Wendell shift into his lap, and motioned for me to join him on the couch, which I did.

Before I let Cosmas apologize for doing nothing wrong, I leaned my head on his shoulder and asked him why it was that I felt so strongly about Wendell and making him happy.

I also told Cosmas that I admired the fact that he had managed to keep a healthy emotional distance from Wendell, and said that I used to think my heightened neuroses when it came to Wendell just showed that I loved Wendell more than him, but now I had to wonder. . . .

Maybe it all meant that I just happened to be crazier than he was. Cosmas shook his head and said that he thought I was wrong—that, in fact, he thought all of my angst when it came to Wendell was strictly just the manifestation of my deep love for our dog. He then reminded me how I could microdissect and overanalyze anything, and that perhaps some of it had to do with just having too big a heart in combination with too much time on my hands. Cosmas then admitted very quietly that perhaps he wasn't such an emotional brick wall when it came to Wendell after all, because the letter had affected him rather deeply and perhaps his whole drama-king couch thing was just his inability to know what to do with those feelings. . . .

Happy simply that my letter had gotten the credit it was due, I smiled at this. I then gave Wendell's sleeping head a pat and said it was time for us all to go back to bed.

Of course, heading back to the bedroom behind Cosmas and Wendell, I couldn't help asking, "So does that mean you *don't* think Santa will bring Wendell a dog?"

🐾 🐾 🐾

I will say that when Cosmas walked in with a big box that he said was an early Christmas present for Wendell, there were trace amounts of jealousy mixed in with the cresting waves of my curiosity. On the one hand, I was pleased that Cosmas had taken it upon himself to get Wendell a surprise present. On the other hand, I tended to favor surprises that either (a) I was responsible for, or (b) were for me. On the third hand (or why not say paw, since we've already run out of hands), I decided to reserve all judgment until I saw the contents of the box, because perhaps it was actually a present I could share in.

Cosmas then quickly explained to me that this wasn't the actual gift for Wendell, and was simply something that he had borrowed from a colleague, but that if Wendell liked his present, he would buy him one closer to Christmas. He then set the box on the coffee table in the living room, opened it up, and pulled out a small white robotic dog. Wendell and I both cocked our heads to the left at the sight of it, but then Wendell leapt up from where he was sitting next to me on the couch and was soon jumping up and down at Cosmas's side.

With my hand over my mouth, I suppressed a giggle and leaned forward as Cosmas set the Sony Aibo dog on the living-room floor. Having been activated by a small button on its underbelly, the little dog sprang to life and a jazzy electronic beat began to emanate from it and it began to do a little dance on the floor. Wendell was now bowing before it with his little furry butt in the air to signify play and was barking up a storm.

This is when everything began to move in *Matrix* slow motion—I mean, Wendell springing straight up like a champagne cork . . . me leaping up from the couch, completely forgetting that I was holding a Diet Coke, the contents of which came sloshing out in every direction . . . Cosmas reacting a split second after Wendell, lunging forward to protect the little dog . . . Wendell now on a downward arc, speeding straight for the Aibo dog, drool flying through the air . . . me registering the Jackson Pollock splatter of Diet Coke on my previously white Oxford button-down . . . Cosmas's mouth open unnaturally wide as he began to scream, "NOOOOOOO . . ." But it was too late. Defenseless, the little ten-pound robot met all forty-five pounds of Wendell as he slammed into contact and they both went skidding and smashing into the living-room wall.

Both Cosmas and I now had our hands clapped over our eyes. There was simply no way that a noise that loud could have been a good thing. Wendell was standing up again and shaking his head, probably trying to get those stars floating before his eyes to stop, but the little robot dog was no longer making any music. Which was probably not the best sign. After a few sniffs, Wendell dismissed the toy as no longer any fun and proceeded to walk out of the room and start lapping up water from his bowl (terminating new kids on the block must make a dog thirsty).

Cosmas moved first, rushing over to the fallen dog, and soon he was kneeling on the floor next to it, moaning something unintelligible. I moved in closer to hear, but only when I was kneeling on the floor right beside him did I understand that he was saying "two thousand dollars" over and over again. It took a few times of my hearing this mantra before it registered, whereupon I chose perhaps the *most* unhelpful response I could have—I freaked.

"TWO THOUSAND DOLLARS? THAT LITTLE WALKING CD PLAYER WAS TWO THOUSAND DOLLARS? WHAT WERE YOU THINKING?"

Cosmas turned toward me with the saddest expression you've ever seen and just said, "I was thinking that maybe this robot dog could act as a placeholder for Wendell until we got him another dog to play with."

I had no response for that, as it suddenly dawned on me that I had in fact been an accessory to this crime.

"Maybe he didn't break it." Always the optimist when my own hide was on the line.

Cosmas just shook his head. "Did you see the way they slammed into the wall? Hell, I'm surprised Wendell is even walking."

I shrugged. "Well, at least rigor mortis hasn't set in yet." Cosmas shot me a dirty look, which was interrupted by Wendell reappearing and barking again at the sight of Cosmas holding the fallen dog in his hands. And these barks weren't in play.

I looked at Wendell and then at Cosmas and then back to Wendell. "Ohmygod, Tony Soprano on a bad therapy day. I don't think he likes it."

Cosmas hurriedly put the Aibo back in its box, mumbling something about assessing the damage later, but I could tell the way his shoulders slumped forward that he was depressed about the whole thing. Here he had taken the time to try to find a solution that would make everyone happy (give Wendell a playmate, have me stop harassing him about

Wendell getting a playmate), and voilà—the whole thing went bust, literally, in less than a minute. Now granted, I didn't quite know how it was he deduced that Wendell would even like a robot dog (though my top three explanations would be that Cosmas *did* go to MIT, he was a sci-fi fan, and robot dogs didn't poop), but I now figured I was going to have to do some damage control when it came to proving why this was not a fair test case, or "simulation," of how Wendell would react to another dog in the house.

By the time I snapped out of my own personal issues with the situation, Cosmas had already taken the box and brought it into my office and had closed the door—out of sight, out of mind.

He was the first to speak. "There's nothing to say. I tried; I failed."

How I loved Cosmas's straightforwardness in such situations. He was right, though, as there was, in fact, nothing much one could say about a dead robot dog. This would just go down in our family history as this one little blip on the screen (well, if we're going with the techno references) and that was all (though I did feel I could speak to anyone who might be paranoid that machines were one day going to take over the planet; my thoughts were that this was doubtful, since Wendell was hardly the toughest dog around). Unaccustomed to having nothing to say, I did the next best thing, which was that I walked over to Cosmas and gave him my biggest and best there-there-don't-fret-that-we-just-blew-two-grand-on-a-robot-dog-that-our-dog-just-wrecked hug, and like always, Wendell came bounding forth and was jumping up to join in. We let him into our little circle, both of us looking down at him, and for the moment he seemed quite happy that it was just the three of us (at least for now)—yes, a fellowship of three, no, not a fellowship, but a family.

The 10 Breeds of Obsessed Dog Owners

The "Ultimate" Owner

These are the owners that all the rest of us (secretly) aspire to be like. These owners love their dogs to the hilt and yet seem incredibly well adjusted and easygoing about it all. Their dogs listen really well and can walk off leash, but even when, every now and again, they break away to chase after a squirrel, the owners understand this is just what dogs do. There is an obvious show of affection that goes both ways, and it's a toss-up to see who loves who more, but then again, they know it's not a competition. And though these owners love their dogs, they also seem to understand that they are in fact, dogs. And the dogs themselves seem to understand this fact, and seem happy that things have worked out this way.

Hey, it's something to work toward, right?

Appendix

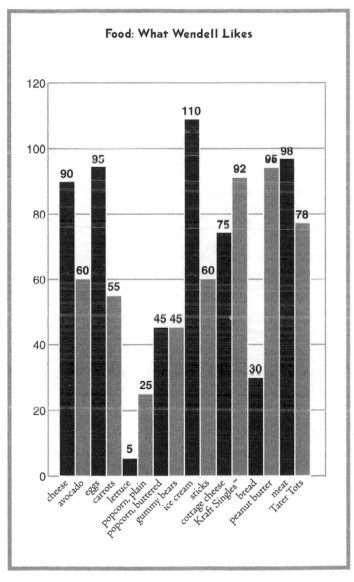

Food: What Wendell Likes

Food	Value
cheese	90
avocado	60
eggs	95
carrots	55
lettuce	5
popcorn, plain	25
popcorn, buttered	45
gummy bears	45
ice cream	110
sticks	60
cottage cheese	75
Kraft Singles™	92
bread	30
peanut butter	95
meat	98
Tater Tots	78

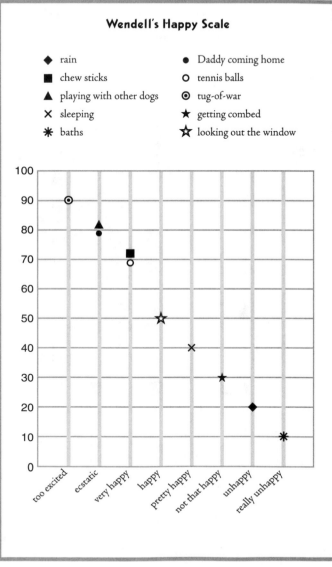

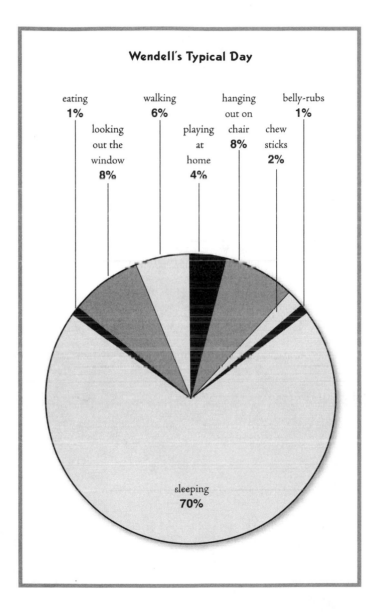

Wendell's Typical Day

eating 1%
looking out the window 8%
walking 6%
playing at home 4%
hanging out on chair 8%
chew sticks 2%
belly-rubs 1%
sleeping 70%

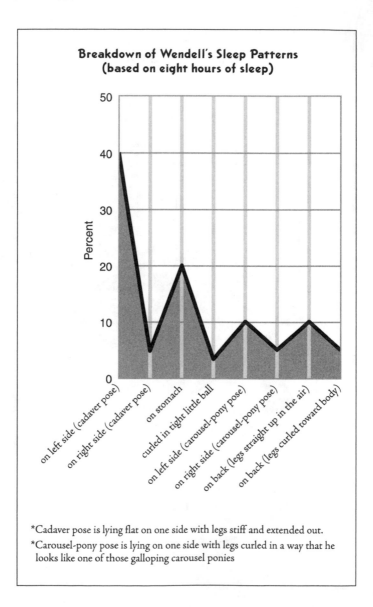

**Breakdown of Wendell's Sleep Patterns
(based on eight hours of sleep)**

*Cadaver pose is lying flat on one side with legs stiff and extended out.

*Carousel-pony pose is lying on one side with legs curled in a way that he looks like one of those galloping carousel ponies

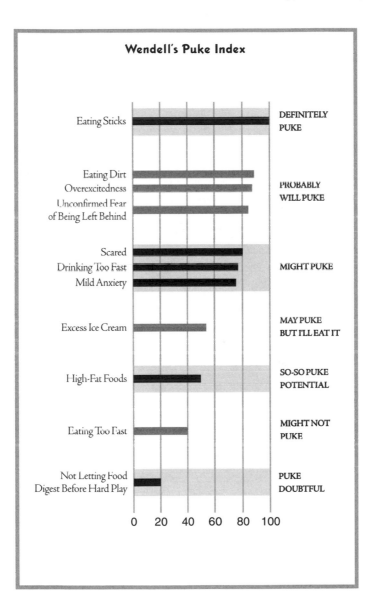

Wendell Elvis Giallourakis
Soft Coated Wheaten Terrier
12 Wendell Street
Cambridge, MA 02138

Wendell12@hotmail.com

Education:
New England Canine University
Advanced Beginners Obedience Degree, June 2002
Puppy Kindergarten, March 2002

Tricks:
Sit, down, roll over, shake (both paws), high five, speak, fetch

Specialty Tricks:
"Bang-bang (with finger gun)"—will play dead
"Through the hoop"—will jump through hula hoop
"Kiss the ring"—will lick/kiss hand (like in *The Godfather*)

Professional Experience:
I am an up-and-coming "media personality" who is currently the focus of *Animal Fair* magazine's humor column (written by my mom, but I pitch her "ideas"). I am also the main character of a book that my mom is writing about my life, which is a sequel to her first book, which was published in January 2003—I'm not in the first book, because it predates me (or so she keeps telling me).

Relevant Skills:
Able to sit quietly and look cute, can fetch crumpled pieces of paper that don't make it into trash can, am good for procrastinating as I'm always happy to sit on anyone's lap and chew on a rawhide, can alert everyone to "weird" noises when they occur, able to sleep anywhere, will gladly accompany anyone outside when running errands, understand pig latin (sorta), and am extremely soft (hence the word *soft* in soft coated wheaten terrier) and accepting of friendly petting.

Other Interests:
Walking around Cambridge, playing with other dogs at Fresh Pond park, eating ice cream at Toscanini's (favorite flavor is strawberry, as I'm not allowed to have chocolate because it could kill me), reading *New Yorker* cartoons, browsing at the Harvard Bookstore, and watching HBO.

PROUST QUESTIONNAIRE:
An Interview with Wendell

What is your idea of perfect happiness?
Eating Toscanini's strawberry ice cream while sitting on my
    parents' bed with the air conditioner blowing in my face.

Which living person do you most admire?
The people who work at Toscanini's Ice Cream shop in
    Harvard Square.

What is the trait you most deplore in yourself?
That I must do my "business" out in the open.

What is your greatest extravagance?
Sitting in Mommy or Daddy's lap and working over a chew toy.

On what occasion do you lie?
When I do the "I need to go potty" bark when I actually just
    want to go outside and see my friends.

What do you dislike most about your appearance?
My light coloring shows dirt, therefore more baths.

Which words or phrases do you most overuse?
Woof.

What is your greatest regret?
That I cannot adjust the air vents in the car, just so.

What or who is the greatest love of your life?
I will say Mommy and Daddy as that will probably get me
    more of my true great love—duh, ice cream.

Which talent would you most like to have?
To be able to discern the difference between jingling keys and jingling dog tags.

If you could change one thing about yourself, what would it be?
Sometimes I wish I could wear a blue collar instead of a red one.

If you could change one thing about your family, what would it be?
I would like a friend to hang out with.

What do you consider your greatest achievement?
That I have trained my mom to do a high five with me and then give me a cookie.

If you were to die and come back as a person or thing, what do you think it would be?
I think being a dog might be amusing.

If you could choose what to not come back as, what would it be?
I would not be a tree, grassy patch, pole, or sandwich baggie, that's for sure.

What is the quality you most like in a man?
The ability to play a good game of tug-of-war.

What is the quality you most like in a woman?
The ability to give a good belly-rub, with just the right amount of rub and oohing-and-ahhing ratio.

What do you most value in your friends?
Stillness while I smell them, sharing toys.

Who are your favorite composers?
Andrea Bocelli is my favorite singer, and my favorite song is
"Hark! The Herald Angels Sing"—as it's the one song my
mommy knows all the words to, and she sings it to me
whenever I'm sick or scared.

Who is your favorite hero of fiction?
Old Dan and Little Ann (*Where the Red Fern Grows*, by
Wilson Rawls).

Who are your heroes in real life?
Mommy and Daddy?

What are your favorite names?
Wendell (said in a friendly tone as opposed to I'm-in-trouble
tone). Boobookins. Wookatdatface.

What is your motto?
If you have cookie, I will come.

WENDELL'S NEW YEAR'S RESOLUTIONS

1. Exercise more (preferably off leash—hint hint)

2. Eat more ice cream, cookies, and Starbucks pumpkin bread

3. Try to kick my bad habit of eating sticks (makes me throw up)

4. Spend more time with friends (maybe start a book club?)

5. Learn how to speak squirrel

6. Finish research and write paper on "Why baths are bad for dogs"

7. Come up with a stupid pet trick for Letterman

8. Try to resolve my issues with "the call of the wild" (therapy maybe?)

9. Give more to charity

10. Practice tricks every day

Wendell's Acknowledgments

I would first like to thank my mommy and daddy (i.e., Jenny Lee and Cosmas Giallourakis) for their constant love and support, because without their daily devotion (the food, the walks, the bellyrubs, and the neuroses) this book would not have been possible. A big bark-out to all my friends: Thatcher, a dog couldn't ask for a better friend; Atticus, no one wrestles better than you; Emma, Lucy, Nina, Alex, Bruin, Jasmine, Clive, Tess, Sophie, bb, Toby, Ambika, Pooch, Jake, Bosco and Barney, Duncan, and all the dogs I play with at Sacramento Park, all the dogs at Fresh Pond, and of course my New York friends at the Union Square dog run. I would also like to give a warm woof-woof in memory of Ebby. I'd also like to say thanks to Aunt Susie and Uncle John, Grandma Lee (who introduced me to Andrea Bocelli), Aunt Carrie and Uncle David (Thatcher's super cool parents and my favorite babysitters), Aunt Victoria and Uncle Jay (Atticus and Nina's parents), Aunt Stephanie and Uncle John

(Emma's parents), Aunt Laura and Uncle Chris (Alex's parents), Aunt Jenner, Aunt Jackie and Uncle Josh, Uncle Phil (thanks for teaching me how to play poker), Aunt Anne and Uncle Alex, Aunt Becky and Uncle Kenny, Aunt Christine O., Aunt Julie and Uncle Ryan, Aunt Lisa, Aunt Cheryl, Aunt Janet, Papou Giallourakis, an extra special loving tribute to my late YiaYia (Antonia) Giallourakis, Aunt Stamie and Uncle Aris, Aunt Christina and my favorite cousins, my pals Alexander and Orry. I would like to give a twenty-one-bark salute to Rob McQuilkin (mine and Mommy's literary agent) whose dedication and countless hours of loyalty and support will always be remembered; also I'd like to give a wink and a woof-woof to Matthew Snyder, my CAA agent (I just love saying that, aren't I cool?), and Jodi, too. My best roll-over salute to Danielle Perez (editor extraordinaire) and everyone at Bantam Dell (especially Nita Taublib, Barb Burg, Shannon Jamieson, and Irwyn Applebaum) for finding me adorable and my stories funny enough to publish, and a big doggy kiss for all their hard work and devotion to help get this book out there. I would also like to thank all those who work with Toscanini's ice cream, the makers of rawhide, the creator of tennis balls, and the employees of Petco and all dog-toy stores in general. Thank you to my groomers—especially Jeanna's Dirty Dog Salon in Cambridge, Massachusetts, and everyone at Porter Square Veterinarians, Cambridge Veterinarians, and VESCONE Animal Hospital, Petersen Thomas for my portrait, Janet of Suis Generis, and all my friends from the Wendell Street book club. High five to *Animal Fair* magazine (especially my first *AF* editor, Jennifer Cattaui). Big woof-woof to everyone who works with dogs, period. If we could talk, we'd all tell you thanks. I'd like to dedicate this book to all obsessed dog owners out there—you're all crazy, but we love you just the same, and of course, we dogs are so worth it!